IMAGES
of Sport

HAMPSHIRE
COUNTY CRICKET CLUB

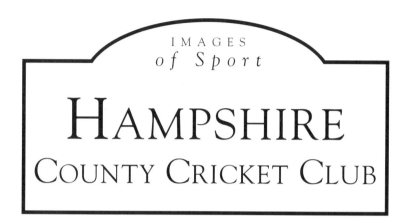

IMAGES
of Sport

HAMPSHIRE
COUNTY CRICKET CLUB

Compiled by
Dave Allen, Neil Jenkinson and Andrew Renshaw

TEMPUS

First published 2000
Copyright © Dave Allen, Neil Jenkinson and Andrew Renshaw, 2000

Tempus Publishing Limited
The Mill, Brimscombe Port,
Stroud, Gloucestershire, GL5 2QG

ISBN 0 7524 1876 9

Typesetting and origination by
Tempus Publishing Limited
Printed in Great Britain by
Midway Clark Printing, Wiltshire

Dedicated to the memory of Malcolm Marshall

Also available from Tempus Publishing

Glamorgan CCC	Andrew Hignell	0 7524 0792 9
Glamorgan CCC 2	Andrew Hignell	0 7524 1137 3
Glamorgan Greats	Andrew Hignell	0 7524 1879 3
Kent CCC	William A. Powell	0 7524 1871 8
Leicestershire CCC	Dennis Lambert	0 7524 1864 5
Scarborough Festival	William A. Powell	0 7524 1638 3
Somerset CCC	Somerset Cricket Museum	0 7524 1585 9
Worcestershire CCC	Les Hatton	0 7524 1834 3
Yorkshire CCC	Mick Pope	0 7524 0756 2
The Five Nations Story	David Hands	0 7524 1851 3

(all books are 128 page softbacks with the exception of *The Five Nations Story* which is a 176 page hardback with colour illustrations.)

Contents

The County Ground in Southampton, showing the pavilion that was built in 1885.

Foreword

When my brother Chris and I arrived at Hampshire in 1981 it was the beginning of a great adventure, which continues to this day.

We joined a side with some very fine players, including Gordon Greenidge, Malcolm Marshall, David Turner and Trevor Jesty, and we knew something of the county through the exploits of Barry Richards.

At that time there were a number of changes at the club which led to Mark Nicholas becoming captain of a team that included some of my great friends, including Paul Terry, Cardigan Connor, Bobby Parks and Tim Tremlett. In 1986 we enjoyed the excitement of winning the Sunday League in a tight match at the Oval and two years later all of Hampshire celebrated when we appeared in our first Lord's final.

Stephen Jefferies was the hero that day, although I enjoyed myself with the bat until my innings was ended by a fabulous catch from Steve Goldsmith. Fortunately, that innings helped to clinch my place in the England side a few years after Chris had made his Test debut.

Although we have had a number of semi-final disappointments over the years, we also enjoyed two further cup final successes in 1991 and 1992 and I was fortunate enough to win the Man of the Match award on both occasions. They were great days for everyone associated with Hampshire.

As we enter a new millennium a number of exciting developments on and off the field give us good reason to be optimistic for the future of Hampshire County Cricket Club. In the meantime this book is a marvellous record of a great club with a great spirit. It will bring back many happy memories – enjoy it.

With best wishes,

Robin Smith

Introduction

The notion that history is the story told by the winner is disproved by the early activities of Hampshire County Cricket Club. In 1863 the efforts of a few country gentlemen and business people attracted only a little support in the county and, although by 1865 membership of the fledgling club had risen to 140, the assets consisted only of two marquees valued at £60 and a scoring box worth only a score of pounds. Five years later the original management gave up in disgust and disappointment. No matches at all were played from 1871 to 1874 and the club had to be reconstituted in 1879. Even when they were established, though only as tenants, at the Antelope Ground at Charlotte Place, Southampton (east of the then town centre), and a few professionals were employed, results did not justify any great enthusiasm.

In the early 1880s the executive extended the fixture list, but the more games the side played, the worse they fared. In 1884 they lost 6 games out of 8 and the following year, when the County Ground was opened by the club, there were 9 defeats in 11 fixtures, so the county was adjudged to have lost first-class status, which it did not regain until 1895, in the wake of Somerset (1891), Derbyshire, Essex, Leicestershire and Warwickshire (1894). F.E. Lacey, H.W.R. Bencraft, E.G. Wynyard and Harry Baldwin, who all rendered distinguished service to the club, came to the front during the period of eclipse. Wynyard, who excelled in all manner of sports, played a major role in assuring the club's promotion, and continued into the front line as long as he was able to play: he was only the first in a long line of sportsmen from the forces, whose service at Aldershot, Winchester or Portsmouth gave a particular flavour to the county's cricket until the mid-1920s – with a decided break over the period of the Boer War (1899-1902), which coincided with another lean period.

When revival came in 1906, the chief contributions were from Badcock, a professional fast bowler, and, more durably, Charles Llewellyn, the South African. They were followed by a succession of young professionals: James Stone, the wicketkeeper who first played in 1900, Alec Bowell (1902), Phil Mead (1905), Jack Newman (1906), Alec Kennedy (1907) and George Brown (1908). The last five each contributed over twenty years' service. By 1912, strengthened by the presence of C.B. Fry, Hampshire had a truly admirable side which finished sixth in the championship that year and fifth in 1914.

At this time, Hampshire could produce enough players to make two first-class sides, selected from: C.B. Fry, A.C. Johnston, C.P. Mead, Capt. E.I.M. Barrett, J. Stone, J. Newman, G. Brown, A. Bowell, Revd W.V. Jephson, H.C. McDonnell, Capt. W.N. White, G.N. Bignell, E.R. Remnant, A.S. Kennedy, E.M. Sprot, H. Hesketh Prichard, A.C.P. Arnold, Hon. L.H. Tennyson, Lieutenant C.H. Abercrombie, A.L. Hosie, A. Jaques, J.G. Greig and W.H. Livsey. This distinguished period continued after the First World War under the captaincy of the ebullient and hard-hitting Lionel Tennyson, just as it had begun when the sardonic and independent- minded Sprot held the team on a tight rein. As the 1920s wore on, the supply of amateurs began to dry up, while one by one the great professionals suffered a loss in effectiveness and dropped out of the side, beginning with Bowell in 1927. By 1934, only Mead and Kennedy remained.

The young professionals who established themselves as successors lacked nothing but the consistent ability to pull together, so only in 1932, when the team finished eighth in the Championship and 1936, when in ninth place, did they make much of a showing. This strain continued for the first decade after the Second World War, in spite of the enthusiastic leadership of Desmond Eagar, who re-established lengthy continuity of leadership from 1946 to 1957 (the captaincy of Sprot from 1903 to 1914 and Tennyson from 1919 to 1933 had been followed by a spell of four leaders in six seasons).

When dramatic improvement came, as it did in 1955, it was heralded by the introduction of Roy Marshall from Barbados, the first of a long line of dynamic high quality players from overseas who joined the club. A roll-call of their names – Roy Marshall, Barry Richards, Danny Livingstone, Gordon Greenidge, Andy Roberts, Chris Smith, Robin Smith and Malcolm Marshall – accounts for much of the success of the side over the last forty-five years, with two blips, one in the late 1970s, and the other a few years before the end of the twentieth century.

In 1961 Roy Marshall scored 2,607 runs at an average of 43 when Hampshire won the County Championship for the first time, but this performance was only part of a marvellous team effort, led by Colin Ingleby-Mackenzie, whose tactics were more subtle than comparisons with Lord Tennyson might have led a casual observer to suspect. This success provided a great climax to the careers of several cricketers, in particular Henry Horton, Jimmy Gray, Leo Harrison, Derek Shackleton and the skipper himself. For Peter Sainsbury, however, that year of glory found a worthy successor in 1973, where he was the only survivor of the 1961 team to participate in the second successful race for the top. Greenidge and Richards shared the batting honours, but Sainsbury came third. He was also the most economical of the six bowlers that earned top place for the side, who, unlike their predecessors, were undefeated.

By 1973, the one-day game had come to stay in the form of the Benson & Hedges Cup, the John Player League and the Gillette Cup. Over the last twenty-five years, Hampshire's principal honours have come in limited-overs cricket: they won the NatWest Trophy in 1991, the John Player (Sunday) League in 1975, 1978 and 1986, and carried off the Benson & Hedges Cup in 1988 and 1992. They have also finished as runners-up or semi-finalists in these competitions on fourteen occasions and have been Second XI champions four times, the last in 1995.

Just as this book was being completed, the authors visited Broadhalfpenny Down on New Year's Day 2000, for the first match of the season, if not the millennium, in the UK. In direct contrast to the experience of New Year's Day 1929 – when frost permeated the ground on which the match between Hampshire Eskimos and the Invalids was interrupted by the arrival of the Hambledon Hunt – on 1 January 2000 the sun shone, the wind dropped and the view of the surrounding landscape was clear and encouraged thoughts of an early spring. Even if that optimism turns out to be unjustified, this year – in which Hampshire will cease play at Northlands Road and move to West End, and which sees the welcome debut of Shane Warne – can only be a memorable one for cricket supporters in the county.

Acknowledgements

In making our choice of the illustrations in this book, we decided as far as possible to use material in the possession of Hampshire County Cricket Club, in order to give the reader some idea of the collection they hold. Much of it cannot at present be displayed for reasons of space.

However, we are also indebted to the following and acknowledge their permission to publish material in this book: Newscom and their librarian Peter Ashton for generous co-operation, Richard Binns, Gary Chalk, Patrick Eagar, Cyril J. Hart, Susanne Marlow and the Hulton Getty Collection. We also thank the following for their help: A.F. Baker FCA (chief executive, Hampshire CCC), Ben Jenkinson, Jean Jones, the librarian for local studies at Southampton Public Library, John May MPS and Brian Scrimshaw.

One
Before the
Championship

Cricket began its development in the Weald, the undulating and formerly well-wooded country in Kent and East Sussex. The earliest reference to a match involving a Hampshire side is dated 1729 and Portsmouth are recorded as playing in 1741 and 1749. The games played by the Hambledon Club over the forty years from 1756 form the first series of important matches anywhere of which we have a detailed record. Here, a match is taking place at Broadhalfpenny Down, Hambledon, in front of the Bat and Ball.

Left: The name 'Hampshire', under which the Hambledon men sometimes played, was used by various teams, as was the title Gentlemen of Hampshire, but there was no settled organisation in the county. One of the best cricketers produced by Hampshire before their first-class days was Thomas Beagley of Farringdon near Alton, who hit 113 not out for the Players against the Gentlemen at Lord's in 1821. *Right:* In 1862, Thomas Chamberlayne and other gentlemen met to discuss the revival of cricket in the county. In the following season, Surrey filled a cancelled fixture with a scratch game against fourteen of Hampshire. This happy accident created sufficient enthusiasm to lead to a general meeting on 12 August 1863 at the Antelope Inn, Southampton, to make preliminary arrangements for the foundation of a county cricket club.

Daniel Day (1807-1887) at the Antelope Ground. Day made his mark as a fast bowler in South London, before moving to Southampton in 1842. Under the patronage of Thomas Chamberlayne of Cranbury Park (near Eastleigh), Sir F. Bathurst and Sir J.B. Mill, he leased the Antelope Cricket Ground at St Mary's, Southampton, which became home to the County Cricket Club in 1864. He subsequently opened another ground across the Itchen at Woolston before moving to the East Hants enclosure in Southsea.

Chamberlayne became president and G.M. Ede (above left) was made the first honorary secretary. Ede was famous as a gentleman jockey and went on to win the Grand National on The Lamb in 1868. Two years later, he was killed when his mount fell on him. His twin, E.L. Ede (above right), a subsequent secretary to the club, lived on to edit the early *Hampshire Cricket Guides*, and to score for the county team after they became first class.

The minutes of the meeting of the club committee on 4 May 1868. This was a dark hour which saw the resignation of Mr Chamberlayne as president and E.L. Ede as honorary secretary because support had fallen and success was scarce. W. Beach and Captain Eccles were their successors.

Hants County Cricket Club 1868
Monday May 4th 1868

A Committee meeting was held this day at the Antelope Hotel – Present
F. Chamberlayne Esq. in the chair
H. G. Green Esq.   B. W. greenfield Esq.
E. L. Ede Esq   C. Lucas Esq.
Capt. Eccles
The acting Hon Sec Mr. E. L. Ede. informed the meeting, that Mr. Beach and Captain Eccles had accepted respectively the office of President and Hon Sec. vacant by the resignation of Mr. Chamberlayne and Mr. George Ede –
Mr. Ede read a letter from Mr. Burnup (the Sec of the Surrey Club) which was in reply to one written by him, at the desire of the Last meeting –
Captain Eccles took over the office of Hon Secretary from Mr. E. L. Ede –
The New Hon Sec was authorized by the meeting, to write and publish a letter Stating, that, The Hants County Club

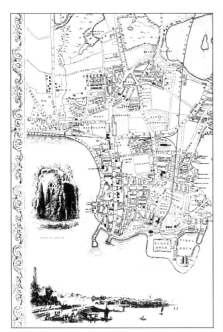

Left: A map showing the site of the Antelope Ground and the future County Ground in Northlands Road, just west of Banister Lodge. *Right:* A more detailed plan of the Antelope Ground.

The county at the Antelope Ground. Here, between 1864 and 1884, Hampshire played 27 matches, of which they won 11 and lost 14. In 1876, W. Mycroft of Derbyshire returned analyses of 9 for 25 and 8 for 78 (17 wickets for 103 in the match). The ground was renowned for its excellent turf: in 1884, the home team hit 645 against Somerset, to which F.E. Lacey contributed a century, following it with 211 and 92 not out against Kent. The county never had security of tenure at the Antelope and moved to Northlands Road in 1885.

For a time the old ground became home to Southampton Football Club (the Saints) but was eventually built over.

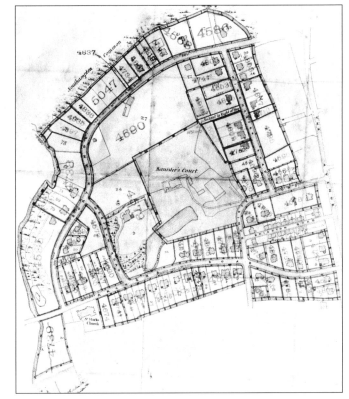

This plan shows the development of the Hulse Estate, including the site of the County Ground (4690 on the map) and of The Dell, home of the Saints (bottom left at 4739). Note the three ponds, which were subsequently filled in.

The County Ground, Northlands Road. Above is the original pavilion built in 1885 and below as it was rebuilt about ten years later. The view from Banister Park School looked like this until 1926, when the school closed, the boundary was fenced and Mr Charles Knott Snr laid out a speedway stadium and greyhound track, subsequently the site of an ice rink, where suburban housing now stands. This ground was, like the Antelope, briefly used by the Saints before they moved to The Dell. The wooden construction to the left of the pavilion was built for their spectators as a grandstand and served the cricket club as a dining room until it was demolished in 1956.

Above left: Captain (later Colonel) James Fellowes (1841-1916). To Captain Fellowes goes the credit for successfully negotiating a lease of eight acres of land on the Hulse Estate in 1883 which, laid down under his supervision, was opened as the County Ground in 1885. He was a very hard hitter and fast bowler, in the old round arm style, who had played for Kent before his military duties brought him to Hampshire. A great organiser, he shared the county's secretarial duties with Russell Bencraft for some seasons. *Above right*: R.G. Hargreaves (1852-1926). Reggie Hargreaves played in 12 matches for Hampshire between 1875 and 1885, scoring 307 runs at an average of 15, with a highest score of 38. He was subsequently a committee member and vice-president for over thirty years up to his death. He has a better claim to fame as the husband of Alice in Wonderland, née Alice Liddell. *Right:* Sir Francis Lacey (1859-1946), whose batting raised Hampshire's standing during the lean years of the 1880s. He first played for the county in 1879 and won his blue at Cambridge in 1882. Apart from his success against Kent, he scored 157 and 50 (and took 11 wickets) versus Sussex at Hove in 1882, and no less than 323 against Norfolk at Southampton in 1887 – still the highest total in a minor county match. In 1898 he became secretary of MCC and revitalised the club.

A.J.L. Hill (1871-1950). For most of the twenty years before the First World War, no Hampshire eleven was complete without Arthur Hill, a tall, stylish batsman and fast bowler (before changing to lobs). His highest score of 199 came against Surrey in 1898 and in 1905 he hit a century in each innings against Somerset. Touring South Africa in 1895/96, he played in three Tests, scoring 124 at Cape Town. In 1921 he appeared with his son, A.E.L., in the Hampshire side.

Dr Henry William Russell Bencraft (1858-1943) was the ultimate enthusiast and meant everything to Hampshire cricket for nearly sixty years. Among the posts he held were honorary secretary (1895-1902), chairman (1908, 1919-1934) and president (1911-1912 and 1935). Bencraft had been captain when the club re-entered the County Championship in 1895 and was a free-scoring batsman. Prominent in many spheres in the county, both sporting and otherwise, he was knighted in 1923.

Two
Into the Championship

Hampshire's spell among the second-class counties ended after nine seasons in 1895. Rival teams had earned promotion the previous year, but Hampshire missed out through lack of form, until they made a sudden advance in August 1894. They beat Essex twice and added Derbyshire, Warwickshire and Sussex as victims, as well as having the better of Leicestershire in a rain-ruined match. With five victories in those six encounters, Hampshire had made their point and they were promoted for 1895. This is the XI which represented the county in their first Championship match that May. Left to right, back row: H. Baldwin, Capt. Barton, G.W. Lewis (scorer), C. Heseltine, T. Soar. Front row: C. Robson, Capt. E.G. Wynyard, Dr R. Bencraft, A.J.L. Hill, H.F. Ward. On ground: F.H. Bacon, V. Barton.

COUNTY CRICKET GROUND, DERBY.

AUGUST 6th, 7th, and 8th, 1894.

DERBYSHIRE v. HAMPSHIRE.

Batsman's No.	HAMPSHIRE.	First innings		Second Innings.	
1	Mr A J L Hill	c and b Davidson	0	b Davidson	6
2	Mr C Robson	b Hulme	1	b Hulme	7
3	Barton	c Wright, b Davidson	1	l b w, b Sugg	29
4	Capt Quinton	c Storer, b Hulme	20	c and b Davidson	17
5	Bacon	c Storer, b Davidson	4	b Sugg	14
6	Mr H F Ward	not out	61	not out	12
7	Capt E G Wynyard	c Davidson, b Hulme	90	not out	9
8	Mr A H Wood	c and b Hulme	5		
9	Mr D A Steele	b sub, b Hulme	10		
10	Baldwin	c Evans, b Davidson	5		
11	Cave	b Hulme	3		
		wds 1 bys 3 lb nb	4	wds bys 4 lb 3 nb 1	8
		Total	204	Total	102

Fall of Wickets.—1st Inns.

1	2	3	4	5	6	7	8	9	10
1	2	9	31	159	176	194	199	204	

2nd Inns.

1	2	3	4	5	6	7	8	9	10
13	13	60	66	91					

Bowler's No.	DERBYSHIRE.	First Innings.		Second Innings.	
3	Mr L G Wright	b Baldwin	86	b Baldwin	2
4	Hulme	run out	24	c Quinton, b Baldwin	0
7	Bagshaw	c and b Hill	5	c Quinton, b Baldwin	10
5	Chatterton	l b w, b Baldwin	11	b Hill	16
1	Davidson	b Baldwin	9	c Robson, b Baldwin	9
2	Storer	b Baldwin	0	b Baldwin	10
6	Sugg W	run out	27	c Hill, b Barton	77
8	Mr F Evershed	b Baldwin	0	c Hill, b Baldwin	19
10	Evans	b Steele	2	run out	23
9	Malthouse	not out	0	c Robson, b Baldwin	4
11	Mr G G Walker	b Hill	6	not out	2
		wds bys lb nb		wds 1 bys 7 lb 2 nb	10
		Total	117	Total	188

Umpires—

G Atkinson & F Coward

Fall of Wickets—1st Inns.

1	2	3	4	5	6	7	8	9	10
45	55	78	75	75	82	84	95	109	117

2nd Inns.

1	2	3	4	5	6	7	8	9	10
17	19	29	82	83	106	139	147	178	188

LUNCHEON *provided at the Grand Stand from* 12 *till* 3, *at* 2/6 *each.*

Printed on the Ground by S. B. Smith, of 24, Back Sitwell-street, Derby. Price 1d

PRINCE OF WALES

ROYAL THEATRE

SOUTHAMPTON.

Benefit Performance

In aid of the Funds

OF THE

Hampshire County

... *Cricket Club,*

FEBRUARY 16TH, 1898.

MRS. NORTON CHILD'S

Pupils' Mandoline, Guitar, and Banjo Band

Will play between the pieces.

E. Roberts, Typ., Southampton.

Above left: Scorecard of the Derbyshire match, August 1894. This was one of the matches against their promoted opponents which regained Hampshire's first-class status in 1895. Wynyard made 90 and Baldwin took 12 wickets. *Above right:* Edward George Wynyard (1861-1936). In the climax to the 1894 season, Captain Wynyard followed his score of 90 against Derbyshire with consecutive centuries from the bowling of Sussex, Leicestershire and Essex. Against Yorkshire at Southampton in 1896, he surpassed his previous triumphs with an innings of 268, and found a place in the final Test against Australia at the Oval.

Fund-raising in 1898. The county benefitted from many similar shows up to 1914.

In 1899, Major R.M. Poore (304) and Wynyard (224) participated in a stand of 411 for the sixth wicket, as Hampshire amassed 672 for 7 wickets against Somerset at Taunton, which remains the county's highest total. Wynyard captained Hampshire from 1896 to 1899, but was often conspicuous by his absence – and not always on military duties.

Somerset County Gazette

GRATIS CRICKET SLIP.

Gazette Office, Castle Green, Friday Evening.

SOMERSET V. HAMPSHIRE.

GRAND BATTING DISPLAY BY MAJOR POORE
AND CAPTAIN WYNYARD.

A RECORD PARTNERSHIP FOR TAUNTON.

THE SECOND HIGHEST IN EXISTENCE.

TO-DAY'S PLAY.

Major Poore and Soar upon continuing the visitors' innings this morning quickly began to improve the condition of things for their side. The major was soon in his stride, and scored freely off Tyler and Gill. The century appeared when the innings, with the time taken overnight, had lasted an hour and 25 minutes. The next item of interest was when Major Poore reached his half-century, for which he had been batting 70 minutes. The score stood at 109, and at 118 Robson bowled for Gill, while two later Cranfield relieved Tyler. Three-quarters of an hour's play had resulted in the overnight score being doubled. Tyler came on again for Robson at 140, and at the same total Robson went to the river end to displace Cranfield. Both batsmen played with the utmost confidence, Major Poore driving and cutting in brilliant manner. Nichols was tried at 156 and Stanley at 175, but the runs still came, and Poore reached his century. This made the third consecutive hundred made against Somerset, and it had taken him just under two hours to compile. Previous to this Soar had made his score 50, the professional having been at the wickets an hour and 20 minutes. The major had added two to his century when he was missed in the slips off Nichols by Robson. The 200 appeared in 2½ hours, the same rate of scoring as on the previous day by Somerset. At 201 Tyler bowled at the river end, and runs came with even greater freedom than before, Soar now being credited with the most of the scoring. The 250 appeared 20 minutes after the 200 had been hoisted. Two from this total Gill bowled at the pavilion end, and Soar skied him into that structure. The change, however, had the desired effect, for at 258, Soar, who had made 95, was caught by Cranfield in the slips off Gill. He had given a chance of being caught at the wicket at 52, and his splendid partnership with Poore resulted in 196 runs being added for the fifth wicket in an hour and 55 minutes. Soar's last 45 runs had been made in 35 minutes, and the chief hits in the contribution were fifteen 4's, three 3's, and two 2's. His previous best score was 85 against Derbyshire this season. Major Poore was joined by Captain Wynyard, and the pair were together at lunch time, the score being 306. The 300 went up in 3½ hours.

A resumption was made at 2.20, and the total of the Somerset innings was quickly passed. Gill and Tyler shared the attack, and the score was taken along at a good rate. Cranfield relieved Gill at 348, and Wynyard soon reached his 50, for which he had been batting an hour and a quarter. Major Poore treated all the bowling alike, and beat his previous best score in county cricket, which was 175, made against Surrey, at Portsmouth, on June 30th. Wynyard made some hard drives and fine cuts off Cranfield, and as a result of vigorous cricket the fourth century appeared when the innings had lasted four hours and three-quarters. Eight later Stanley bowled at the river end, and Major Poore turned his attention to the new bowler to the tune of three 4's and a single, which caused his total to reach 200. Robson and Tyler came on

again, and 4's were the order of the day, Wynyard hitting a ball from the left-hander to leg on to the roof of the cottages. Captain Wynyard caused no little amusement by attempting a back s roke to a delivery of Tyler, which, however, did not succeed. At 4.15 the captain also gained the distinction of scoring a century, which had taken him two hours and 25 minutes. He had been 10 minutes scoring the three necessary to complete the century. The score stood at 461, Poore being not out 216, and Wynyard not out 106, when ten was taken.

After a quarter of an hour's interval, the game was resumed, Gill and Nichols bowling. A separation did not seem likely, the bowling apparently lacking sting, while the batting was a fine exhibition of driving and cutting. At 497 Tyler bowled for Gill, and immediately afterwards Wynyard brought up the 500 off Nichols. The innings had progressed five hours and 50 minutes. With the score at 529 Cranfield bowled for Nichols, and as a result of this change, a separation should have been effected for Capt. Wynyard drove the new bowler high to the long-field, where Bernard received the ball in his hands but failed to hold it. In Cranfield's next over Wynyard raised his total to 150, his innings then having lasted three hours and a quarter. Variation to the continuous scoring was seen by Mr. Robson carrying out stone gingers to the batsmen and fielders. With his total at 158 Wynyard gave a difficult chance of c & b to Cranfield, but the hit was an exceedingly hot one. The same stroke, and following this 550 up with the same bowler, and following this Wynyard hit Cranfield up against the pavilion scoring box. Daniell was given a trial at the pavilion end, and in one over Wynyard drove him hard and low to Tyler at mid-off, who failed to make the catch. The captain's score stood at 170 at this juncture. The 600 was signalled in six hours and three-quarters, the last hundred having taken only fifty-five minutes to score. Some 20 runs on Gill made a good attempt to catch Wynyard at mid-on from a hard drive. At ten minutes past six Wynyard had claimed his double century, which had taken him four hours to compile. The crowd now awaited the signalling of Poore's third century, and the Major should never have reached it, for at 293 he was badly missed at backward point off Tyler. The stand came to an end at 6.25, having lasted four hours and twenty minutes, by Wynyard being caught at over-point off Tyler. For the sixth wicket 411 runs had been added, and this beats all records except that for the first wicket of 554 scored in August last by Brown and Tunnicliffe for Yorkshire against Derbyshire. Although the exhibition was marred by chances it was nevertheless a fine innings, and in it were included two 5's, thirty-six 4's, six 3's and seven 2's. Curiously enough, with Baldwin in, Tyler in the same over caused the dismissal of Major Poore, who had been in six hours and 50 minutes for 304.

Harry Baldwin (1860-1935) was a slow-medium right-arm bowler, with a well-controlled off-break and a ball which went with the arm. Baldwin, eighteen years after his debut, was perhaps a little past his best by 1895, but he returned a series of outstanding performances, finishing with 102 wickets in Championship matches at 16.13 each. He never achieved such heights over a season again, but headed the county bowling averages as late as 1904. His benefit match against Yorkshire in 1897 was over in one afternoon, as Hampshire collapsed for totals of 42 and 36.

A Nottinghamshire man, Tom Soar shared the bowling honours of 1895 with Harry Baldwin. His fast bowling, which was well supported by the fielders behind the wicket, brought him 89 victims at an average of 18.60, including 7 wickets in an innings on three occasions. Subsequently, he was never so fit or effective again and his failure to maintain his early form contributed to the team's decline in 1900 to 1904.

PRICE ONE PENNY.   HAMMETT & CO., PRINTERS, TAUNTON.

SOMERSET COUNTY CRICKET GROUND,
TAUNTON, JULY 20th, 21st & 22nd, 1899.

Somerset v. Hampshire.

SOMERSET.	First Innings.		Second Innings.	
1 H. T. Stanley	b Soar	28	c Steele b Heseltine	9
2 C. A. Bernard	c Robson b Heseltine	42	c Steele b Baldwin	7
3 Robson	b Soar	74	run out	19
4 R. C.-N. Palairet	c Robson b Soar	29	run out	27
5 J. Daniell	c Robson b Baldwin	0	c Lee b Baldwin	57
6 Nichols	b Baldwin	64	c Lee b Wynyard	13
7 Gill	c Steele b Heseltine	8	c Webb b Wynyard	6
8 A. E. Newton	c Robson b Wynyard	46	c Steele b Baldwin	33
9 Tyler	not out	15	c English b Baldwin	10
10 Rev. A. P. Wickham	b Wynyard	1	not out	0
11 Cranfield	absent	0	b Wynyard	3
	l-b 7, n-b 1	8	B 19, l-b 1, w 2	22
	Total ..	315	Total	206

1-63 2-81 3-159 4-164 5-194 6-204 7-290 8-309 9-315 10-
1-16 2-26 3-63 4-78 5-98 6-114 7-189 8-199 9-206 10-206

HAMPSHIRE.	First Innings.		Second Innings.	
1 C. Robson	c and b Tyler	15		
2 Barton	l-b-w b Tyler	12		
3 Major Poore	st Wickham b Tyler	304		
4 E. A. English	b Gill	0		
5 E. C. Lee	c Nichols b Cranfield	11		
6 Soar	c Cranfield b Gill	95		
7 C. Heseltine				
8 Capt. Wynyard	c Bernard b Tyler	225		
9 Webb	not out	2		
10 D. A. Steele				
11 Baldwin	not out	1		
	l-b 3, w 4	7		
	Total....	672*	Total....	

1-26 2-31 3-38 4-62 5-258 6-669 7-670 8-   9-   10-
1-   2-   3-   4-   5-   6-   7-   8-   9-   10-

Umpires—Pickett & Burton.   Scorers—S. McAulay & G. W. Lewis.
Interval at 1.30 p.m.   Stumps Drawn at 5.30 p.m.
* Innings declared closed.

Major Robert Montague Poore (1866-1938). Six feet four inches in height and largely self-taught as a batsman, Poore followed a good first season with phenomenal performances in 1899, when between 12 June and 12 August he scored 1,399 runs in only 16 innings, with an average of 116.58. His first three innings were 104, 119 not out and 111. On four other occasions he exceeded a hundred and he surpassed even his own high standard with 304 not out in his great partnership with Wynyard.

Above left: Some of Poore's performances are recorded on the scorecards shown above, which come from his own collection. His military career prevented him playing in more than a handful of matches. He consoled himself with success in the numerous other sports in which he excelled and in his military career – he retired as a Brigadier-General. *Above right:* J. Stone (1876-1942) was the first Southampton professional to earn a county cap. He was the regular wicketkeeper from 1900 to 1913 and scored 1,000 runs in 1911, 1912 and 1913. He was fortunate in the timing of his benefit against Yorkshire in 1912, which immediately followed Hampshire's famous win over the Australians, when interest in the county was at fever pitch. Displaced by Livsey behind the stumps in 1914, he played for Glamorgan in 1922/23 before becoming a first-class umpire.

Edward Apsey English (1864-1966). In his second game for the county, in 1898, he saved the game against his native Surrey with what turned out to be his highest score for Hampshire. He did not maintain this start, but deserves a place in the county's history as the second most long-lived first-class cricketer, having been born only four months after Hampshire County Cricket Club was founded.

Centenarian cricketer's innings ends

"*Echo*" Staff Reporter

THE world's oldest first-class cricketer Mr. Edward Apsey English, who has died at his daughter's home near Tiverton in his 103rd year, appeared in 15 first-class matches for Hampshire CCC between 1898 and 1901 and was the county's senior ex-player.

He was also the only English first-class cricketer a centenarian. F. A. Macklinson who played for Cambridge University and Kent, died in 1947, two months short of his 99th birthday.

A native of Dorking, Surrey, where his father was a builder, Mr. English was educated at the local Grammar School and in his teens made a reputation in the local club side as a fast bowler.

5 FOR 12

For the Young Players of Surrey against the full Surrey side at the Oval, in 1883 he took five wickets for 12 runs—a performance which many expected would lead to a cricketing career. But Surrey, then richly endowed with bowlers, refused to give him a trial and it was not until he moved to Alton as Registrar of Births and Deaths in 1896, and joined the Alton CC that his ability won recognition.

In 1898 he made his debut as an amateur for Hampshire against Lancashire at Old Trafford. In his second game, against his native county, at the Oval, he made his highest score, 98, saving a game that was to all intents and purposes lost, by a courageous display on a difficult wicket against the two best fast bowlers of the time, Lockwood and Richardson.

His performance in that game won him his county cap but apart from a 60 against Essex at the County Ground, Southampton the following summer (top score in an innings of 266) he achieved little of note for his adopted county.

GOLF AND SNOOKER

But after his county cricket days were over he played for Alton CC until he was 66; then took up golf and in his 83rd year, off a handicap of 12, holed the 180 yard ninth hole on the local course in one. He also played in an Alton Golf Club side which won a national competition.

A great billiards and snooker player, it came as no surprise to members of the Alton Conservative Club, when he cele-

World's oldest cricketer dies

Oldest first-class cricketer in the world, Mr. Ted English, who played for Hampshire at the turn of the century, has died, aged 102.

brated his 93rd birthday by playing in the final of the club's snooker competition. The fact that he was beaten, by a man half his age, did not deter him from agreeing the following year.

In 1962 after living over 60 years in the town, and achieving a reputation as Alton's best known and best-liked personality, Mr. English moved to Cadleigh near Tiverton, South Devon, to live with his daughter, Miss Esther English, who after running a WLA hostel at Newton Vallence, Alton, during the Second World War took up farming in Devon.

"Ted" English as he was universally known, was quite the most remarkable character I ever met and certainly the most extraordinary centenarian I have interviewed.

I had corresponded with him for a number of years before, just after his 102nd birthday, I visited him at his daughter's home.

FANTASTIC MEMORY

Apple-cheeked, bearded, he utterly belied his great age by his remarkably alert mind, and a fantastic memory of sporting events that had occurred 80 years earlier.

A great Hampshire cricket enthusiast, I remember he was born only four months after the county club was formed: he was one of the first to send them a congratulatory telegram when they won the championship for the first time in 1961, and he also contributed to their centenary appeal.

His immaculate, copperplate handwriting, legacy of his Registrar days, will be remembered by a host of friends in the north of the county where, as a young man, he played cricket, for only with conspicuous success, but also to enjoy it.

He was an honorary life member of the Alton Constitutional and Golf Clubs, a Freemason and showing his interest even after he had notched a "ton" of birthdays, a vice-president of Buckingh (Devon) Cricket Club. He had promised to open their new pavilion last spring—and did so.

His wife, to whom he was married 57 years, died in 1946. He leaves a son, who lives in America, and two daughters.

Last April, when he was 102 years and 104 days old he became the oldest ex-player in world cricket history. F. Wheatley of Canterbury, who died in 1889, aged 102 years and 103 days.

Above left and below: Hampshire versus the South Africans, 1901. The Boer War was still being fought when the magnate from the Cape, J.D. Logan, brought over a team from South Africa. Their results overall were satisfactory, but the team's reputation never recovered from an overwhelming defeat at the hands of Hampshire. *Above right:* Charles Bennett Llewellyn (1876-1964). Llewellyn, who contributed so much to Hampshire's victory, was himself a South African, representing his country 15 times between 1895 and 1912. In 1901 he played on occasions for his home team as well as Hampshire. His figures for the season were 1,025 runs at an average of 31.06 and 134 wickets at 22.53 each. In 1902 this left-handed all-rounder also achieved the double, which he did again in 1908 and 1910, after which, following a dispute with the county over terms, he joined his compatriots on their tour of Australia and played in Tests in 1910, 1911 and 1912, before extending his career in league cricket.

Hampshire against Sussex at Brighton, 1904. This was one of the heaviest defeats in a season when the county were last in the Championship for the first time in five years. Sussex scored 508 for 9 to win by an innings. This is a rare picture which shows Poore as captain in the absence of Sprot; the only appearance that year of D.M. Evans; Hayter, a professional trialist; J.H. Bacon, the club secretary; and Harry Baldwin, who had been recalled after two years' retirement to strengthen the bowling. From left to right, back row: C.B. Llewellyn, A. Webb, W. Langford, H. Baldwin, A. Bowell, Hayter. Front row: J. Stone, F.H. Bacon, Major R.M. Poole, D.A. Steele, D.M. Evans.

Edward Mark Sprot (1872-1945). As captain between 1903 and 1914, he built up a cohesive team, based on a core of professionals: Stone, Llewellyn, Bowell, Mead, Newman, Brown and Kennedy. Sprot himself was a hard-hitting, middle-order batsman and an imaginative leader who kept tight control over his team. He scored 12,212 runs for Hampshire between 1898 and 1914. It was a good day for the county when he joined them, having moved south from Scotland during a spell in the Army.

No. 13, VOL. I. SATURDAY, JUNE 27, 1914. PRICE 3D.

Hampshire's Captain.

In his forty-third year, his sixteenth season of first-class cricket, and his twelfth campaign as captain of the Hampshire eleven, E. M. Sprot has played in successive matches a couple of innings equal to anything he has ever accomplished; and that is saying a good deal.

The innings referred to are, of course, his 86 v. Kent at Tonbridge and his 131 v. Surrey at the Oval. The latter is his thirteenth century for the county and his first since 1911.

At Tonbridge he and Philip Mead stood in the breach when a complete collapse seemed likely, and added 149 for the sixth wicket after five had fallen for 54. At the Oval matters were worse, for Mead had gone for a duck, and five were down for 43. Sprot found helpers in Haigh Smith and the lengthy Jaques; but they merely stayed while he made runs, and his 131 bulked more than common large in a total of only 239, of which 12 were extras.

Probably no other amateur who has played so much county cricket as E. M. Sprot has played so very little first-class cricket outside his county's games. He has appeared (up to June 20) in 259 matches for Hampshire, and in exactly three matches (South v. Australians, 1902; Gentlemen of South v. Players of South, 1903 ; and Hambledon v. England, 1908) ranking as first-class besides !

Seldom, too, has any cricketer stepped into a county team and done well from the start who was so little known to the general public as was Sprot in 1899. He was in the Army then (the 85th Regiment, now the 2nd Battalion Shropshire Light Infantry), and had been making runs in plenty for the United Services' team at Portsmouth ; he scored 176 for U.S. v. Hampshire Hogs in 1898. In the red *Lillywhite* his name appears in the Century List as " Sprot " ; and for some seasons after he had become well known the scorers would occasionally give him the " tt " to which he does not lay claim. By the way, he aroused one particular scribe's facile enthusiasm by pointing out that he was *not* " Major E. M. Sprot " ; additional cause for admiration might have been found, possibly, in his dispensing with an affix as well as a prefix to which he was not entitled !

Born at Edinburgh on February 4, 1872, Edward Mark Sprot was at Harrow in the days of A. C. MacLaren and the Hon. F. S. Jackson ; but his cricket did not develop early, and, like H. P. Chaplin (another ex-Army man), in later years he failed to get his flannels.

23

"Together joined in Cricket's manly toil."—*Byron.*

No. 39. VOL. II. New Series. SATURDAY, MAY 24, 1913. [Registered at the G.P.O. as a Newspaper.] PRICE 2D.

A Chat about Alec Bowell.

ADVENTITIOUS circumstance sometimes gives to a man fleeting hour of fame. He may have done many things every whit as worthy as that which brings him for the me being into the limelight; but that is no matter. Certain facts have a way of striking the public mind; and the fact that Bowell has scored the first century of his season in county cricket has made him more talked than he ever was before. He has scored other centuries. This is his tenth for Hampshire. This one had distinct merit, both as to execution and on account of a fact that it was not one of a number of big innings, and Brown making practically all the runs for their side; but he has played others quite as meritorious. Alec Bowell—the "Alec" his own version, and I do not know whether he is entitled to the more sonorous and formal "Alexander" was born in Oxfordshire, April 27, 1881, and joined the ground staff of Southampton when only seventeen. Before leaving his native county he frequently played with Huggins and Langdon, both now of Gloucestershire, and also with "Razor" Smith of Surrey. He first represented Hampshire in 1902, and made 44 v. Derbyshire at Derby on his initial appearance. His only other innings worth mentioning that season was 43 v. Leicestershire at Leicester; and in 1903, when he played pretty regularly, he

only once topped 50, making 61 v. Leicestershire at Leicester. He came more to the front in 1904, when his highest score—95—was made v. Somerset at Taunton, and was the best for his side in the innings, as was his 65 against the South Africans at Alton, and, again, his 65 v. Sussex at Hove. Without doing big things, he showed in this season a real capacity for playing an up-hill game; and one innings of his in which this was specially noticeable was his 42 v. Kent at Tonbridge. The wicket was queer, and the Kent bowlers are not just those one would choose to meet on a damaged pitch; the total was 85 (4 extras), and Bowell's score was 42, the next highest being 16 by G. D. Katinakis, who helped him to add 46. His first century came in 1905, after a succession of 20's and 40's. It was against Derbyshire at Southampton, and he followed it up with 51 in the second innings. His 59 v. the Australians was the highest score in his side's second innings, too. He was constantly making useful scores that season, and, without any phenomenal feats, was doing one man's share in the marked revival of Hampshire cricket which the last decade has witnessed. In 1906 his best innings was 74 v. Leicestershire at Leicester, the highest for his side in the match. His

A. BOWELL.

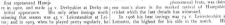

Above left: Alec Bowell (1881-1957). This was a rare headline for this steady batsman and fine cover point between 1902 and 1927. Bowell came from Oxfordshire and was awarded a benefit in 1913. His highest score of 204 came against Lancashire in 1914, but his finest feat came almost at the end of his career in 1926 when, with Hampshire needing to make 508 to win or bat all day for a draw, he (132) and Phil Mead (177 not out) added 248 for the fourth wicket in 3 hours 50 minutes. *Above right*: Captain C.A.R. Hoare. Pictured in 1906, Captain Hoare was the principal supporter of the club up to his death in 1908 and president from 1905 to 1908. He was also the founder and backer of the naval training school, HMS *Mercury*, on the River Hamble, where tight control was exercised by Hoare's mistress, Beatrice Holme Sumner (who became the wife of C.B. Fry). Ironically, it was after Hoare's death that Fry transferred his allegiance from Sussex to Hampshire, to enable him to play a greater part in the running of the school.

Colonel J.G. Grieg (1871-1958). A soldier in the Indian Army and latterly a Roman Catholic priest, Grieg was immediately successful on his debut in 1901 when his neat and elegant batting played a big part in Hampshire's temporary promotion to seventh place in the Championship. His five centuries included 119 against the South Africans and 249 not out against Lancashire at Liverpool. In 1905 he scored a century in each innings against Worcestershire and continued to show good form (while on leave) until 1922, when he became the county secretary. He was president in 1945/46.

F.H. Bacon (1869-1915). Francis Hugh Bacon hit a century for Hampshire against Warwickshire at Edgbaston on his debut in 1894, but the match was not first class. It was thirteen years before he hit a second one, versus Leicester in 1907. After playing as a professional up to 1903, he turned amateur on his appointment as the county's first paid secretary, and was one of the few cricketers of his time to play in both capacities. Serving as assistant paymaster in the First World War, he was drowned on 31 October 1915 when his ship was mined. In the picture he is seated to the left of Captain Hoare. A very young Phil Mead is behind him and J.R. Badcock, who flourished briefly as a fast bowler in 1906 and 1907, is to the rear of Hoare.

George Smoker (1881-1965) first played for Hampshire in 1901, but only once hit the headlines when in 1907 he captured 7 South African wickets for 35. On the strength of this, he moved to Merseyside and became professional with the New Brighton Club, where in 1910 he hit over 1,000 runs and took over 100 wickets. Capped by Cheshire, he later moved to Colne in the Lancashire league and subsequently became coach to Birkenhead School. His father, also George Smoker, played for Hampshire in 1885.

COUNTY CRICKETERS.

G. SMOKER,

HAMPSHIRE.

Charles Burgess Fry (1872-1956). A superstar of the twentieth century who excelled at soccer, rugby and athletics, as well as cricket, Fry had already played 17 tests for England and, as a Sussex player between 1894 and 1908, had exceeded 2,000 runs in a season six times (and topped 3,000 as well) before the first of his 44 appearances for Hampshire in 1909. Because his performances were spread over seven seasons up until 1921, he has never received proper credit from county supporters. In 1912, Fry led England to success in Tests against Australia and South Africa, and he averaged 58.90 for 3,829 runs for the county. The highest of his career total of 94 centuries was 258 not out for Hampshire against Gloucestershire in 1911.

The team which beat the Australians in 1912. From left to right, back row: E.R. Remnant (twelfth man), J. Stone, J. Newman, G. Brown, C.P. Mead, H.A.W. Bowell, A.S. Kennedy. Seated: G.N. Bignell, C.B. Fry, E.M. Sprot, E.I.M. Barrett, Revd W.V. Jephson. Every member of this side hit a century in first-class cricket. This was the last victory by a county over the Australians until 1956.

Hampshire at Bournemouth, August 1912. From left to right: H.A.W. Bowell, A.S. Kennedy, J. Stone, Capt. W.N. White, Capt. E.I.M. Barrett, E.M. Sprot, H.C. McDonnell, G.N. Bignell, G. Brown, C.P. Mead, J. Newman. This eleven played low-scoring games between 26 and 31 August at Bournemouth in a wet week in 1912 against Nottinghamshire and Surrey. Surrey's 78 gave them a lead of one on the first innings, but Hampshire, in turn, declared at 68 for 8, leaving 40 minutes for play. Hayward and Hobbs had reached 28 in half that time when rain intervened. Hampshire dismissed Warwickshire for 58 and knocked off the 63 to win in 35 minutes. Bignell's 41 not out in the first innings was the highest score for Hampshire in the week. He made many useful runs between 1904 and 1925. McDonnell was a crafty slow bowler for Hampshire over a similar period and W.N. White was yet another hard-hitting Army cricketer.

The Golden Jubilee of the club in 1913 was celebrated by a week of cricket at Southampton, starting on 16 June. Both games were closely contested, Surrey winning by five runs, while at the end of the Nottinghamshire match the visitors needed eight to win, with two wickets in hand. C.P. Mead scored 127 in the second innings total of 221 in 2 hours 20 minutes. On 17 June, the club held a banquet at which Lord Harris proposed 'success to the Hampshire CCC', to which the club president, J.C. Moberley, responded.

A section of the crowd at Northlands Road during the Jubilee: straw boatered, attentive and respectful.

J.C. Moberley was president from 1913 to 1918. He was in the Winchester College XI in 1866 and played once for the county in 1877. Later he was their honorary treasurer and then chairman of the committee.

Hampshire take the field against Nottinghamshire during the Golden Jubilee. From left to right (two figures hidden): Stone, Bowell, H. Hesketh Prichard, Kennedy, Mead, Jaques, J.S.R. Rutherford, Sprot, Newman.

H. Hesketh Prichard, Sprot and Jaques about to take the field against Surrey. Prichard, who took 100 wickets in all matches in 1904, was an author and explorer who died at an early age.

Arthur Jaques (1888-1915) was a great might-have-been of cricket, who was killed in action in France in September 1915. He had been married earlier that month and left a legacy to the club. After a moderate first season, he became an important member of the attack in 1914 when, as vice-captain, he captured 112 wickets at 18.26. *Wisden* described his methods thus: '6 feet 3 inches in height, he placed nearly all his field on the onside, and pitched on the wicket, or outside the leg stump, and swinging in with an off-break, cramped the batsmen so much that many lost patience and succumbed.'

The Long Man of Hampshire.

Hampshire, 1914. From left to right, back row: W.H. Livsey, J.H. Down, A.S. Kennedy, G. Brown, H.A.W. Bowell, J. Newman. Front row: J. Stone, H.A. Haig Smith, A. Jaques, J.G. Greig, C.P. Mead. Livsey displaced Stone as wicketkeeper in this season, though Stone was still played on occasions for his batting. This was also the season that contained Down's only Championship match. He is believed to have been an Australian, but there are no further details. H.A. Haig Smith was an enthusiastic amateur who played when other amateurs were not available.

Hampshire XI, Bournemouth Cricket Week, 1913. From left to right: W.N. White, Hon. L.H. Tennyson, A. Jaques, H.C. McDonnell, C.H. Abercrombie, J. Stone, G. Brown, A.S. Kennedy, H.A.W. Bowell, C.P. Mead, J. Newman. This was a strong Hampshire team of the period, although the absence of Kennedy for the first part of the season was a handicap. Abercrombie scored 920 runs at an average of 38 during this season and, with George Brown, added 325 for the seventh wicket against Essex. However, naval duties prevented him playing in 1914 and he was killed at Jutland a year later.

Three
Between the Wars

Two major forces in Hampshire cricket: Jack Newman (left) and the Hon. Lionel Tennyson, with forty-six years of service between them.

PLAYER'S CIGARETTES.

HON. L. H. TENNYSON,
HAMPSHIRE.

Lionel Tennyson (1889-1951). Few cricketers of the inter-war period are so affectionately remembered as the Hon. Lionel Tennyson, grandson of the poet, who succeeded Sprot as captain in 1919. He did not possess the tactical skill of his predecessor, but lacked nothing in courage or gusto. The early years of his captaincy, like the latter years of Sprot, form one of the most successful periods in the history of the club. He captained England in three Tests against Australia in 1921, echoing the gallantry he had shown with the Rifle Brigade in the First World War, with courageous innings of 63 and 36 at Headingley.

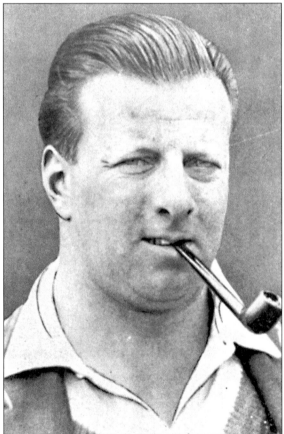

Lord Tennyson, as he became in 1928, at a charity game during the Second World War. After giving up the captaincy before the 1934 season, he continued to play until the end of the following year. He added to his long experience of overseas tours when he headed a team to India in 1937/38.

Hampshire at Leeds, 1920. This eleven defeated Yorkshire at Leeds by an innings and 72 runs. George Brown and Alec Bowell put on 183 for the first wicket, while Brown went on to the highest score of his career, adding 271 for the third wicket with Mead. The scores were: Hampshire 456-2 declared (G. Brown 232 not out, C.P. Mead 122 not out, A. Bowell 95); Yorkshire 159 (H. Sutcliffe 58, A.S. Kennedy 6-69) and 225 (P. Holmes 78, W. Rhodes 64). On a wicket which suited them, Kennedy took 10 wickets for 135 and Newman 6 for 110 in the match. The players are, from left to right, back row: J. Evans, H.D. Hake, J. Newman, W.H. Livsey, F. Ryan. Front row: G. Brown, A.S. Kennedy, Capt. E.I.M. Barrett, Hon. L.H. Tennyson, C.P. Mead, H.A.W. Bowell.

The pavilion, *c.* 1920. This fine view shows the northern end of the former football stand to the left, which was used by cricket spectators as a dining room until 1956. On each side of the main pavilion are the small, balconied dressing rooms which originally stood on each side of the first single-storeyed headquarters. The left-hand one is, at the time of writing, the oldest building on the ground.

Scorecards for sale from the printer, in the den beneath the dressing room.

Hampshire against Kent at Southampton in 1921. Hampshire won by 131 runs. The scores were: Hampshire 336 (Tennyson 98, Fry 96, Mead 61, F.E. Woolley 5-89) and 200 (Woolley 5-64); Kent 191 (J. Seymour 57, Kennedy 5-63) and 214 (G.C. Collins 93). This was Lieutenant. O.W. Cornwallis' only match for Hampshire and his brother, Capt. W.S. Cornwallis, represented Kent (who he subsequently captained). Both retired from the game after the first day, as their elder brother had been shot in Ireland. From left to right, back row: G. Brown, H.A.W. Bowell, C.P. Mead, J. Newman, A.S. Kennedy, W.H. Livsey. Front row: Lieutenant O.W. Cornwallis, A.L. Hosie, Hon. L.H. Tennyson, C.B. Fry, Capt. E.L. Armitage.

Ronald Aird was a fine batsman for Eton, Cambridge and Hampshire from 1920, who later became secretary of the MCC.

Warwickshire versus Hampshire at Edgbaston in June 1922 has been described by John Woodcock as 'the most wonderful example of the glorious and everlasting uncertainty of our favourite game'. Cricket's greatest comeback saw Hampshire bowled out for 15 and, following on, struggling to clear the 208 arrears with six wickets down. They eventually achieved a total of 521 and then dismissed Warwickshire for 158 to gain the most improbable of victories by 155 runs. Only a team comprising strong characters could have pulled off such a turnaround. Tennyson's never-say-die attitude was paramount and the hero, George Brown, who scored 172, was never more dangerous than when the odds were steeped against the team. Walter Livsey rose to the occasion magnificently with a maiden century when his captain and employer most needed his unstinting service. Brown and Livsey put on 177 for the ninth wicket in only 140 minutes. The last wicket pair of Livsey and Stuart Boyes added another 70, leaving Warwickshire a target of 314. Kennedy and Newman bowled them out for 158. The victorious Hampshire team consisted of, from left to right, back row (excluding umpires): G. Brown, W.H. Livsey, G.S. Boyes, W.R. Shirley, A.S. Kennedy, J.A. Newman. Front row: H.A.W. Bowell, A.S. McIntyre, Hon. L.H. Tennyson, H.L.V. Day, C.P. Mead.

Above: An aerial view of the County Ground in 1926. Northlands Road has changed little since 1897, when the ladies' stand was erected, and 1956, when the office block replaced the old football stand. However, by the end of the twentieth century almost every detail surrounding the ground had been obliterated by housing – as will the ground itself at the end of the 2000 season. This view includes the semi-rural aspect of Banister Park. *Below*: Another view looking across to Banister Park.

Hounds stop play. Cricketers celebrated New Year's Day in 1929 with a match on Broad-halfpenny Down, Hambledon, which was interrupted by the hunt.

'Suits you, sir!' Hampshire's game against Nottinghamshire at Southampton in May 1930 ended in farce when Hampshire needed just one run to win after the extra half hour had been played on the second day and Nottinghamshire's captain, Arthur Carr, refused to continue. The next morning the Nottinghamshire players took the field in suits and overcoats, and Kennedy hit Carr's second ball to the boundary for victory by five wickets.

Presentation to Lord Tennyson, 1936. Tennyson last played for the county in 1935. Hampshire made a presentation to him of a silver cigar box during the match against India in August 1936. A.J.L. Hill, chairman of the club, is to the bottom right of the photograph and Dick Moore, in whites, is to the left, with Neil McCorkell in pads at the rear. The recipient could not conceal his disappointment that the box was empty!

A dinner was held in honour of Sir Russell Bencraft in 1937. The great and the good assembled at Southampton's 'Ritz' – the South Western Hotel – to honour the sixty years' association between Sir Russell Bencraft and the club. The speakers were Col. C. Heseltine, the club president; Col. The Right Hon. Sir Stanley Jackson, the Yorkshire and England cricketer, government minister and Indian governor; P.F. Warner ('Plum'), one of the greatest figures in English cricket; H.D.G. Leveson-Gower, another former England cricket captain; Sir Francis Lacey; and, though not on the toast list, Phil Mead. From left to right, back row: Revd Father J.G. Greig, W. Findlay (secretary, MCC), R.H. Moore, W.G.L.F. Lowndes, P.F. Warner, R. Aird (assistant secretary, MCC). Front row: Sir Francis Lacey, Sir Russell Bencraft, Col. C. Heseltine, Col. Sir F.S. Jackson, H.D.G. Leveson-Gower.

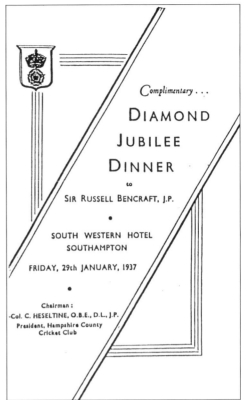

Complimentary . . .

DIAMOND
JUBILEE
DINNER

to

SIR RUSSELL BENCRAFT, J.P.

•

SOUTH WESTERN HOTEL
SOUTHAMPTON

FRIDAY, 29th JANUARY, 1937

•

Chairman :
Col. C. HESELTINE, O.B.E., D.L., J.P.
President, Hampshire County
Cricket Club

Dick Moore, a product of Bournemouth Grammar School, was the most promising newcomer of the early 1930s. He first came good when standing in at Bournemouth for the indisposed Phil Mead in August 1933, scoring 159 in less than four hours against an Essex attack which included three England bowlers. In 1934, still aged under twenty-one, he hit over 1,500 runs and his horizon seemed boundless. Alas, he missed almost all the 1935 season through scarlet fever and did not regain his form until the second year of his captaincy in 1937. After that, business curtailed, then ended, his career before he was twenty-six.

Dick Moore set a county record highest score when he made 316 in a single day against Warwickshire at Bournemouth on 28 July 1937. The sea breezes on that day must have been exhilarating, since along the coast at Hove, Eddie Paynter hit 322 for Lancashire against Sussex. Moore's innings, which included 43 fours and 3 sixes, overtook Brigadier-General Poore's 304 achieved in 1899. The General was not at Bournemouth to see his record broken – he was playing cricket elsewhere. Moore batted faultlessly for 6 hours 20 minutes.

Dick Moore receives congratulations from Brigadier General Poole (left) and Colonel C. Heseltine, the county's president, on the day after his great innings.

A report describing Dick Moore's great innings against Warwickshire in 1937.

R. H. MOORE'S HUGE INNINGS

BREAKS HANTS RECORD WITH 316

FIRST IN, LAST OUT

R. H. MOORE, the Hampshire captain, scored nearly twice as many runs as he has ever made in one innings before, beat the county record, and completed his 1,000 runs for the season, when he punished the Warwickshire bowlers for 316 at Bournemouth yesterday.

He began hitting boundaries almost at once. Eight 4's were included in his first 50, and he reached three figures by pulling the last ball before lunch for 6. His score then was exactly 100, scored out of a total of 147.

Strangely, Moore was an hour adding 19 to his score after lunch, but then he soon began to open his shoulders again. His straight drives, cover-drives and leg-hits travelled at great speed, and he also made some beautiful late cuts.

McCorkell, Creese and C. G. A. Paris gave their skipper excellent support, Creese scoring even faster than Moore while they were together. He, too, hit Hollies for 6.

Moore was first in and last out, as soon after he was lbw to Hollies, the ninth wicket to fall, Boyes had to retire owing to a recurrence of the knee injury which recently kept him out of the game for six weeks. So Hampshire were recorded all out 509.

Moore's previous highest score was 159. The county record stood to the credit of Gen. (then Major) R. M. Poore, who, in 1899, made 304 against Somerset.

HAMPSHIRE

R. H. Moore, lbw, b Hollies	316		Walker, c Kilner, b Hollies		2
McCorkell, lbw (n), b Mayer	33		Hill, st Buckingham, b Paine		0
Creese, b Paine	43		Boyes, retired hurt		8
Arnold, lbw, b Paine	15		Heath, not out		2
C. G. A. Paris, b Hollies	75		B &, l-b 2		10
Pothecary, c Wyatt, b					
Santall	8		Total		509
Herman, c Croom, b Hollies	1				

WARWICKSHIRE: R. E. S. Wyatt, Kilner, Croom, Hill, Dollery, Santall, Mayer, Hollies, Ord, Paine and Buckingham.

HAMPSHIRE.—First Innings

	O.	M.	R.	W.		O.	M.	R.	W.
Mayer	25	4	90	1	Santall	11	0	56	
Wyatt	11	2	51	0	Paine	32	7	97	
Hollies	49.5	9	205	4					

45

C.P. Mead (1887-1958). Phil Mead provided the backbone of Hampshire's batting for thirty years until his retirement in 1936. His total of 48,892 runs for the county is still the highest total by any batsman for any club. He scored 2,000 runs in a season eleven times, exceeding 3,000 twice in 1921 and 1928. However, his more attractive contemporary, Frank Woolley of Kent, was often preferred to Mead, who appeared in only 17 Tests, spread over seventeen years. The highest of his 153 centuries was 280 not out against Nottinghamshire at Southampton in 1921.

George Brown (1887-1964) has claims to being the most complete all-rounder the game has known. As a left-hand batsman, he could lead the charge as an opener or bat anywhere in the order, whilst he was also a hostile fast bowler, whose strength allowed him to bowl long spells. Renowned as a fielder at mid-off, he was understudy to Livsey as Hampshire wicketkeeper but wore the 'keeper's gloves for England in 7 Tests. Any aspect of his Hampshire accomplishments of 22,962 runs, 602 wickets, 485 catches and 50 stumpings might be coveted by a specialist in any department of the game.

Alec Kennedy (1891-1959). Along with Jack Newman, he formed a bowling partnership that bore the brunt of the Hampshire attack. Kennedy, a medium-pace bowler, used swing, cut and finger-spin allied to an unerring length to ensnare 2,874 victims – only four bowlers in the history of the game have taken more wickets. He also scored 16,483 runs, five times completing the seasonal 'double' of 1,000 runs and 100 wickets between 1907 and 1936.

Jack Newman (1883-1972) was a bowler born in Southsea. He spun his off-breaks sharply, but could also swing the new ball. Reverting to spin, he used a well-concealed quicker ball to provide Mead with a steady supply of slip catches. In his career, between 1906 and 1930, he took 2,033 wickets and scored 15,333 runs – matching Kennedy's five 'doubles' – but England passed him over.

Walter Livsey had dual roles as a wicketkeeper and valet to Tennyson. Appropriately known for his neatness behind the stumps, he held 376 catches and made an amazing 255 stumpings. Originally a tailender, he scored a hundred when it most mattered in the 1922 match against Warwickshire, and thereafter was capable of opening the innings if required.

G.S. Boyes (1899-1973). Stuart Boyes was a tall, slender slow left-arm bowler, who became a useful bat with two centuries to his credit late in his career. He captured 100 wickets in a season three times, the best being a return of 111 victims in 1933. He was the only county professional to win a county cap between 1914 and 1929. His best bowling performance was 9 for 57 against Somerset at Yeovil in 1938.

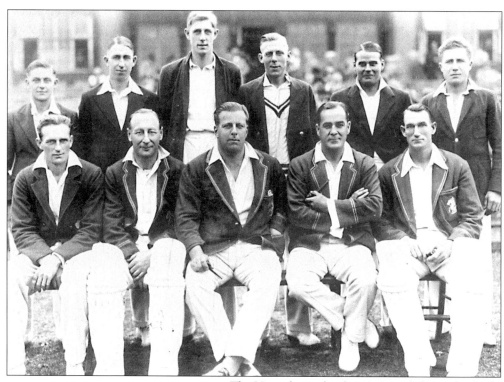

The Hampshire side of 1932. From left to right, back row: N.T. McCorkell, W.L. Creese, O.W. Herman, A.E. Pothecary, J. Bailey, J. Arnold. Front row: G.S. Boyes, C.P. Mead, Lord Tennyson, A.S. Kennedy, G. Brown. This team achieved the best season's results of Lord Tennyson's later years as captain. In spite of a late decline they finished eighth in the Championship, the team's highest finish between 1926 and 1955. The attack of Kennedy and 'Lofty' Herman, at fast-medium pace, and Boyes and Bailey, slow left-arm, was largely responsible. Neil McCorkell replaced George Brown behind the stumps for this season. Note the England blazers proudly worn by the four stalwarts in the front row. Stuart Boyes was also an MCC tourist.

Neil Thomas McCorkell from Portsmouth brought certainty and sprightliness to the role when he replaced George Brown as wicketkeeper in 1932, and the figures of all the bowlers improved as a result. By 1935 he had progressed from a defensive role to an opening batsman, who was not far from Test selection by 1938. However, the nearest he came to international cricket was a tour of India with Lord Tennyson's side in 1937/38. After the Second World War he became a more prolific run-getter, but yielded up the gloves to Leo Harrison and others.

The next six pictures feature Hampshire versus the Australians at Southampton on 23, 24 and 25 May 1934. The players here are, from left to right: G.S. Boyes, C.P. Mead, W.L. Creese, N.T. McCorkell.

A.F. Kippax and S.J. McCabe go in to bat.

From left to right: Pothecary, Arnold and the Hampshire captain Lowndes.

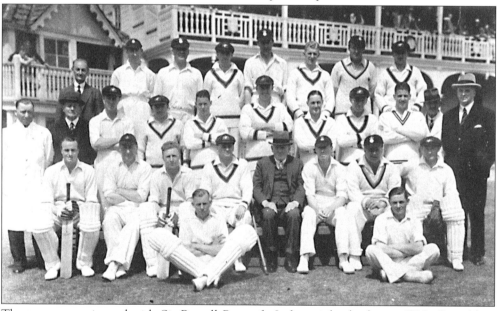

The two teams pictured with Sir Russell Bencraft. Left to right, back row: W.L. Sprankling (Hampshire scorer), W.L. Creese, A.S. Kennedy, A.G. Chipperfield, G.S. Boyes, B.A. Barnett, A.E.G. Baring, S.J. McCabe. Middle row: D. Henden (umpire), G.H. Muir (HCCC secretary), E.H. Bromley, D.G. Bradman, W.A. Brown, W.J. O'Reilly, L.S. Darling, A.F. Kippax, L.O.B. Fleetwood-Smith, W. Reeves (umpire), H. Bushby (Australian manager). Front row: R.H. Moore, C.P. Mead, J. Arnold, W.M. Woodfull, Sir Russell Bencraft, W.G. Lowndes, Lord Tennyson, W.A. Oldfield. On ground: A.E. Pothecary, N. McCorkell.

W.M. Woodfull, the Australian captain, Lord Tennyson and W.A. Oldfield, the Australian wicketkeeper.

Don Bradman and the Australian manager, Mr Bushby. In both 1930 and 1938 Don Bradman went to his 1,000 runs by the end of May during the tourist games at Southampton. In 1930 it was raining and so Newman sportingly tossed up two balls which Bradman hit to the boundary to reach 1,001 runs, whereupon the players immediately left the field. In 1938 rain washed out the first day's play and it was not until the third day on 27 May that Bradman finally scored a century and completed his 1,000 runs – but it remains the earliest date by which the feat has been accomplished. In the 1934 match Bradman was dismissed for a duck. Sir Don has been an honorary life member of Hampshire.

Hampshire in 1937, when Dick Moore was captain for the year. From left to right, back row: N.T. McCorkell, G. Hill, W.L. Creese, H.M. Lawson, W.R. Lancashire, W.L. Budd, A.G. Holt. Front row: A.E. Pothecary, G.S. Boyes, R.H. Moore, J. Arnold, O.W. Herman. Phil Mead dropped out during the previous winter in his fiftieth year. This team includes two sparkling players: Creese, a left-handed all-rounder who only just missed the double in 1936, and Sam Pothecary, a left-hand bat with many handsome strokes (but vulnerable outside the off stump). Arthur Holt was, like John Arnold, a Southampton footballer and became the county's long serving coach. Lawson and Budd were medium-pace bowlers who did not establish a place in the team. Budd became a Test umpire.

John Arnold (1907-1984). Johnny Arnold was from Oxford and a double international whose single Test match for England came in 1931, his second full season. A wonderful summer's batting in 1934 did not bring further selection and after that his seasonal performances were competent rather than great, but he represented quality in the county's batting between the retirement of Phil Mead and the maturity of Neville Rogers. Arnold excelled in the field at cover point or in the outfield. He was one of the generation whose careers lost six seasons because of the war.

Hampshire take the field at Trent Bridge in May 1936. From left to right: W.L. Creese, G. Hill, W.L. Budd, N.T. McCorkell, E.A. Pothecary, J. Arnold, G.S. Boyes, C.P. Mead, H.M. Lawson, O.W. Herman, R.H. Moore (captain). This was Mead's last season as he was not re-engaged early in 1937, when he was about to complete his fiftieth year, but still headed the batting averages. The county were third in the Championship in mid-July but afterwards went to pieces to finish ninth.

Born in 1914, Charles Knott was a bowler of medium line and length deliveries, coupled with sharp off-spin. He first appeared in 1938 and took 9 Gloucestershire wickets in his third match. In 1939 he was a great boost to a faltering Hampshire attack – whenever business allowed him to play – and showed what maturity he had achieved by capturing 8 for 85 against Surrey. His greatest days were to come in the decade after the war.

56

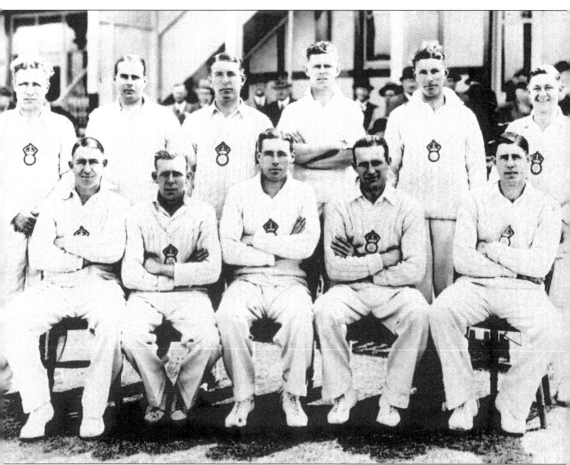

Hampshire, 1938. Cecil Paris was captain at this time and his ten supporting professionals represented a formidable body of talent. Nine members of this team hit centuries in first-class cricket and eight achieved 1,000 runs in a season, while Herman and Heath (fast-medium), Boyes, Creese and Bailey (slow left-arm), and Hill (off-breaks), represented a formidable array of bowling talent. However, in this year they seldom gave their best in unison.

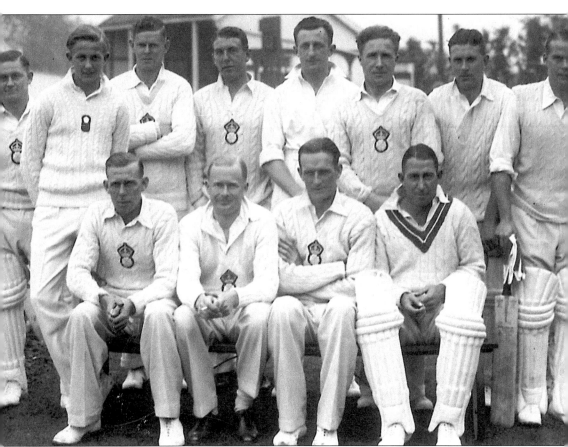

Hampshire at Worcester in May 1939. From left to right, back row: N.T. McCorkell, L. Harrison, G.E.M. Heath, D.F. Walker, A.G. Holt, J. Arnold, G. Hill, J. Bailey. Front row: A.E. Pothecary, G.R. Taylor (captain), G.S. Boyes, W.L. Creese. Pilot Officer Walker was killed when flying over Holland in June 1941, but the others in the back row continued their careers after the war. George Taylor loyally took on the captaincy when Cecil Paris had to return to his law firm in 1939. Leo Harrison's prime did not come until the 1950s. This team of all the talents fared even worse than in 1938 in this last season before the Second World War.

T.A. Dean, born in 1920. In his second county match in August 1939, aged eighteen, Tom Dean took four wickets in five balls (including a hat-trick) against Worcestershire at Bournemouth. At the end of the same week he caused a collapse against Yorkshire, taking 5 wickets for 8 runs, twice dismissing batsmen with two consecutive deliveries. After the war, the county seldom made enough runs to justify his inclusion in the team. Nevertheless, he held seven catches in the match against Essex at Colchester in 1947 – still a Hampshire record. After playing in Devon, he returned to South Africa, where he had spent his youth, and pursued a successful coaching career.

G.R. Taylor, H.S. Altham, E.D.R. Eagar and C.G.A. Paris watch the cricket. Taylor and Paris captained Hampshire in the two seasons before war was declared. Eagar was then playing for Gloucestershire, but was appointed captain and secretary by Hampshire before the 1946 season when first-class cricket began again. Altham and Paris would both become presidents of the county and, with Eagar, were the architects of their great successes of the 1960s and 1970s.

Four
Rebuilding the Side

Aldershot in 1948. Hampshire played a week at the Army ground, the last two of five visits to that venue. They were honoured by the visit of Field Marshall Montgomery, seen here with the Hampshire side, from left to right, back row: Dick Court, Gray, Rogers, Shackleton, G. Dawson, H. Dawson, Harrison. Front row: Hill, Bailey, E.D.R. Eagar, A.N.E. Waldron, Arnold, Heath. The two Dawsons were not related. Waldron, an Army officer, only played in these two matches, whilst Shackleton and Gray made their first-class debuts during the week.

Five players who had returned from the war were awarded a joint benefit over three seasons from 1948 to 1950. The five were Neil McCorkell, Gerry Hill, 'Lofty' Herman, Jim Bailey and Johnny Arnold. Each received £1,470.

Hampshire in 1948 – note the assortment of sweaters! From left to right, back row: Dick Court (secretary), Burden, Harrison, Holt, Heath, G. Dawson, Dean, Rogers, Shackleton, Gray, Taylor, H. Dawson. Front row: Arnold, C.J. Knott, E.D.R. Eagar, Bailey, McCorkell. On ground: Hill, Prouton. Knott, Bailey, Rogers and Holt are wearing the sweater with the Hampshire crest.

Above and below left: Jim Bailey was the last man to do the 'double' for Hampshire when he completed the feat in 1948 at the age of forty. He is pictured here walking out to bat at Portsmouth with Desmond Eagar. *Below right:* Neville Rogers came from Oxford in 1939 but did not make his debut until 1946. Despite the break of six seasons, he was one of the finest post-war batsman never to win a Test cap. Here he is seen opening the batting with Neil McCorkell, who made his debut in the side of Tennyson and Mead.

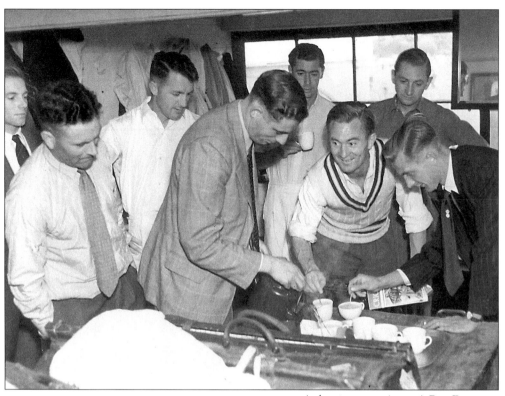

A dressing room 'cuppa': Reg Dare, Vic Cannings and Leo Harrison put sugar in the teas. 'Shack' has his already while Alan Rayment, Gerry Hill, Neville Rogers and Cliff Walker wait in anticipation.

'Holt's Colts'. Arthur Holt became coach in 1949 and developed a generation that would bring Hampshire their first Championship. Here, he is with Malcolm Heath, Peter Sainsbury and Dennis McCorkell (Neil's son).

Three of 'Holt's Colts' take the field after tea at Bournemouth. They are Mervyn Burden, Peter Sainsbury and Mike Barnard.

Harry Altham, Desmond Eagar and Arthur Holt encouraged the development of home-grown cricketers. As a part of their efforts they organised lunch-time coaching demonstrations on the County Ground. This picture was taken during a traditional Whitsuntide match against Kent and shows the old stadium in the background.

Roy Marshall impressed everyone with a century in his first match at Southampton for the West Indies tourists in 1950. With Test opportunities limited he joined Hampshire in 1953 and qualified to play in 1955. Here he practises a cover drive while the trialist at first slip strikes an interesting pose.

A match against Northamptonshire showing the separate pavilions and old office block as well as an absence of advertising hoardings.

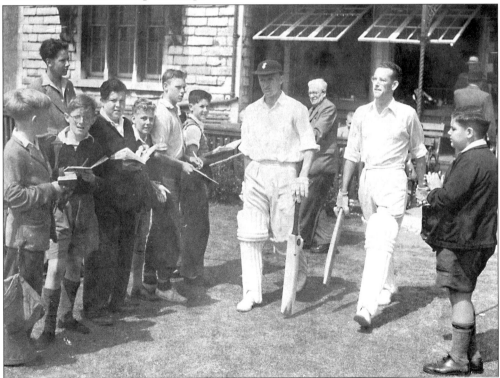

In 1955, Roy Marshall and Jimmy Gray established one of the finest opening partnerships in Hampshire's history. Here they are walking out together at Portsmouth.

A huge crowd watches Hampshire batting against the 1956 Australians. In the background is the Avenue side of the ground and the orchard, later replaced by flats.

Five
Towards the Title

Desmond Eagar's side at Bournemouth. Colin Ingleby-Mackenzie, to Eagar's right, would succeed him as captain in 1958. In 1955 Eagar took Hampshire to third place in the Championship in their Diamond Jubilee season – at that point the highest position they had achieved throughout their history.

Hampshire versus Surrey, 1957. Surrey were in the process of winning the sixth of their seven consecutive Championships, although Hampshire chased them hard in 1955 and 1958. Here the two captains, Desmond Eagar and Peter May, socialise before the match at Portsmouth.

Desmond Eagar leads the side out at Portsmouth in 1957. From left to right: Shackleton, Harrison, Rayment, Eagar, Horton, Cannings, Sainsbury, Heath, Gray.

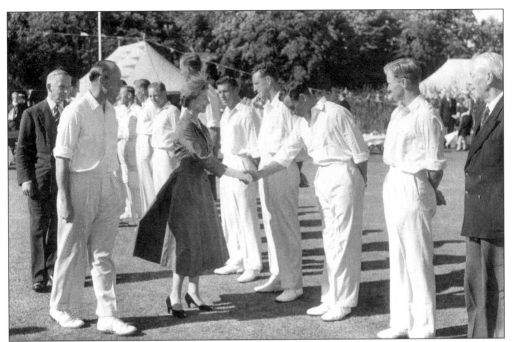

Her Majesty the Queen meets the Hampshire side at Guildford in 1957 as part of local civic celebrations. She is accompanied by Lord Tedder (president of Surrey CCC) and Desmond Eagar, who did not play in the match. The players are: Burden, Horton, Heath, Sainsbury, Barnard (shaking hands), Gray and Hampshire's scorer, Norman Drake.

Cricket at Portsmouth in the 1950s. The church and stand have since been demolished and the skyline is dominated by university buildings. Portsmouth has been Hampshire's most successful home ground.

Hampshire finished second for the first time in their history in 1958, Colin Ingleby-Mackenzie's first season as captain. The players are, from left to right, back row: Sainsbury, Pitman, Rayment, Heath, Burden, Horton, Barnard. Front row: Shackleton, Harrison, Ingleby-Mackenzie, Marshall, Gray. Cannings was also a leading player but is missing from this photograph.

The next four photographs feature Hampshire cricketers who have also played professional football. Henry Horton (with David Blake) joined Hampshire from his summer break as a Southampton full-back.

Mike Barnard (above right) appeared in more than 100 matches for his native Pompey in the old Division One of the Football League and Bernard Harrison (below left and right) is seen here in Hampshire colours and playing for Crystal Palace. Besides the multi-talented individuals shown here, Jimmy Gray was on Arsenal's books.

Derek Shackleton leads a mixture of first and second eleven players in a benefit match in 1958. The players are, from left to right, back row: Bernard Harrison, Stride, Pitman, Timms, Roper. Front row: White, Gray, Flood, Shackleton, Eagar, Barnard.

In Hampshire, the 1960s were dominated by the county's first Championship in 1961. The success owed much to Colin Ingleby-Mackenzie's style of leadership, which had more to do with brilliant man-management than to the well-publicised philosophy of wine, women and song. In addition, Hampshire relied less on declarations than is often believed and won as many matches in 1961 as any other side by dismissing the opposition twice.

Derek Shackleton remained Hampshire's leading bowler through most of the decade and retired with a record 2,669 wickets for the county. In 1963 he opened the bowling for England in their home Test series against Frank Worrell's West Indies side.

Hampshire's Championship was built on effective opening partnerships with bat and ball. Here, Roy Marshall and Jimmy Gray are pictured opening the innings. Both players also contributed useful wickets and the speed of Marshall's runs increased the attacking effectiveness of the side.

Vic Cannings retired after the 1959 season and 'Butch' White established himself as the fastest English bowler in Hampshire's history. He was the perfect complement to Derek Shackleton in 1961 and throughout the 1960s, and was unlucky to win just two Test caps on a tour of India and Pakistan in the winter after the Championship was won by Hampshire. The umpire in this marvellous action portrait is Johnny Arnold, another Hampshire Test cricketer.

Marshall, Gray and Horton gave a very professional start to any innings, but Hampshire's middle-order had often let them down throughout the post-war period. Danny Livingstone arrived from Antigua in 1959 and was the final piece in the jigsaw which turned the 'pretenders' of 1955 and 1958 into the champions of 1961. In the following year he made his highest score of 200 against Surrey at Southampton, sharing a ninth-wicket record partnership of 230 with Alan Castell.

Hampshire won an important victory against Gloucestershire at Portsmouth thanks to some big hitting from 'Butch' White. Here, he drives a ball from England off-spinner John Mortimore, watched by wicketkeeper Barry Meyer, Arthur Milton and non-striker Derek Shackleton.

The County Champions and a large Southampton crowd for the match against Australia in 1961. From left to right, back row: Arthur Holt (coach), Sainsbury, Wassell, Heath, White, Livingstone, Barnard, Baldry. Front row: Burden, Gray, Marshall, Ingleby-Mackenzie, Leo Harrison, Shackleton, Horton. On ground: Bernard Harrison, Timms. The Harrisons were not related.

Bournemouth, 4.30 p.m. on Friday 2 September 1961. Danny Livingstone has just caught Bob Taylor off the bowling of Peter Sainsbury and Hampshire are County Champions for the first time in their history. Colin Ingleby-Mackenzie shakes hands with Mervyn Burden, watched by his team.

The dressing room celebrations after the victory over Derbyshire which clinched the title. From left to right: Colin Ingleby-Mackenzie, Leo Harrison, Danny Livingstone, Derek Shackleton, Alan Wassell, Mike Barnard, 'Butch' White.

A picture which reminds us that Derek Shackleton arrived at Hampshire as a promising batsman and fell just short of 1,000 runs in his first full season. Here he is watched by three spectators and three fielders, including the future England captain Mike Brearley fielding at mid-wicket for Middlesex.

Six

Changing Times

When Bob Cottam established himself in Hampshire's side in the early 1960s the county fielded the finest pace attack in their history. Shackleton, White and Cottam all played for England and in 1965 bowled out Yorkshire for just 23 runs at Middlesbrough. In the same year Cottam took 9-25 against Lancashire at Old Trafford. In this photograph he is enjoying a success against Gloucestershire.

Geoff Keith was born in Hampshire but moved to his home county team from Somerset. Here he hits out against Derek Underwood bowling to four close fielders. Keith later coached the county but died tragically young in 1975.

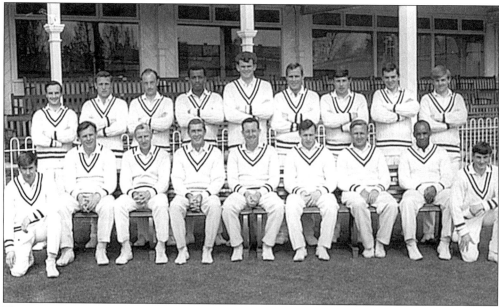

The amateur and professional distinction was officially abolished before the 1963 season, although Colin Ingleby-Mackenzie remained Hampshire's last 'amateur' captain until he retired at the end of 1965. Roy Marshall replaced him and is seen here with his first squad, a transitional side including seven of the first County Champions and three young players – Jesty, Turner and Lewis – who would join Sainsbury in the next Championship winning side in 1973. The full squad consists of, from left to right, back row: Reed, Timms, Caple, Holder, Cottam, Keith, Castell, Wheatley, Jesty. Front row: Lewis, White, Horton, Shackleton, Marshall, Sainsbury, Harrison, Livingstone, Turner.

Hampshire's second XI strike interesting poses in 1967, perhaps in celebration of winning their Championship for the first time. The players are, from left to right, standing: Castell, Barnard, Lewis, Greenidge, Horton, Wheatley, Jesty, Keith. On ground: Leo Harrison, Wassell, Holder. This was Greenidge's first second XI match.

English domestic cricket underwent three major changes in the 1960s. The first was the creation of a single group of 'players', then a knock-out cup and one-day league were introduced, while in 1968 the registration rules were altered to allow the immediate signing of an overseas player. Hampshire's original choice was Clive Lloyd, but when Lancashire beat them for his signature they turned to the brilliant young South African batsman Barry Richards. For ten years he batted with as much skill as any Hampshire batsman can ever have shown in all forms of the game. Only Richards and C.B. Fry have a career average for the county which exceeds 50.

Roy Marshall retired at the end of the 1972 season. In twenty seasons with Hampshire he scored over 30,000 runs at 36 per innings – the second highest aggregate in the county's history. He passed 1,000 runs in a season 17 times and for twenty-six years he and Jimmy Gray held the Hampshire record for the first wicket (249 versus Middlesex at Portsmouth in 1960). Despite these records, he will be remembered more for the flamboyant manner of his batting, bringing a Caribbean flavour to Hampshire in the days before the instant registration of overseas players. He led the county from 1966 to 1970, but for such an exciting cricketer he was a surprisingly defensive captain.

Left: Marshall was replaced as captain by the left-handed Oxford blue Richard Gilliat. He was a reserved, undemonstrative man who nonetheless had the capacity to get the best from a rebuilt and fairly disparate side. From 1973 to 1975, Gilliat led the most successful team in Hampshire's history. He was also assistant secretary until 1978 but, having led Hampshire to a second Sunday League title, he left the club unexpectedly. He is now a school teacher. *Right:* Off-spinner Charlie Knott was the finest amateur bowler in Hampshire's history. He retired at the end of the 1954 season but in the late 1960s replaced Cecil Paris as chairman of cricket. He spent over twenty years in charge, during which Hampshire won a second Championship, three Sunday League titles and appeared in their first successful Lord's final. In 1999 he still attended Hampshire matches regularly and was a member of the Heritage sub-committee.

Seven
Champions Again

Many of the successes of Gilliat's side were built on the start provided by Gordon Greenidge and Barry Richards, not simply the finest opening pair in Hampshire's history but possibly in the history of county cricket. Their achievements and the manner of their execution were extraordinary in Championship and one-day cricket. Only C.B. Fry betters Richards' county average of 50.50 while Greenidge is on a par with the Smith brothers, just behind the top two. Given their skill and the nature of their batting, it is extraordinary that neither man appeared in a one-day final with Hampshire.

Hampshire won their second Championship in 1973 and another key factor in their success was the close catching. Here wicketkeeper Bob Stephenson catches Derbyshire's last man Bob Swindell off the bowling of Peter Sainsbury. Hampshire won this match at Portsmouth by ten wickets.

In the following match in mid-August, first-placed Hampshire met their nearest challengers Northamptonshire and in a low-scoring match beat the Midlands county in two days. Here, Gordon Greenidge is catching Roy Virgin to give David O'Sullivan the first of four wickets in a match-winning spell. O'Sullivan took 37 wickets in the last six matches from the start of August, playing a big part in the county's success. Surprisingly he was not given a contract for the following year.

A huge crowd attended the first day of the Northamptonshire match at Southampton. By lunchtime they were in excellent spirits as they watched Hampshire's seamers Bob Herman, Tom Mottram, Mike Taylor and Trevor Jesty dismiss Northamptonshire for just 108 in 44 overs. At 111-1, just after tea, Hampshire seemed in complete control, but 'Nelson' struck as Bedi dismissed Richards and restricted Hampshire to a lead of 59. Mottram, Taylor and O'Sullivan routed Northamptonshire again and Richards took Hampshire to a vital seven-wicket victory.

The County Champions. From left to right, back row: Lewis, Herman, Mottram, Taylor, Greenidge, O'Sullivan. Front row: Turner, Richards, Gilliat, Sainsbury, Stephenson, Jesty. Hampshire were undefeated and won ten matches in the Championship.

Richard Gilliat celebrates the Championship with supporters and members of his team at Bournemouth on 30 August 1973. From left to right: Turner, Herman, Stephenson, Jesty, Mottram, Gilliat, Sainsbury. Peter Sainsbury is the only man to have appeared in both Championship-winning sides, whilst Turner is the only man to have won Championship, Sunday League and Lord's final winners' medals with Hampshire.

Hampshire were the first side to be awarded the new Lord's Taverners' Championship Cup, which was presented by the Duke of Edinburgh at Buckingham Palace during the winter. The Duke enjoys a joke with Peter Sainsbury watched by Gilliat, Mottram, Herman, Stephenson and Lewis. A Surrey captain lurks enviously in the background.

Hampshire's Championship captains, Colin Ingleby-Mackenzie and Richard Gilliat, at the dinner to celebrate the 1973 success. They are joined by Cecil Paris, at various times Hampshire's captain, chairman, cricket chairman and president.

In 1974, Hampshire released O'Sullivan despite their Championship success because they were able to call on the breathtaking pace of Antiguan Andy Roberts. In his first season he took 119 wickets at 13.62 and created fear across the country.

Hampshire were more dominant in the 1974 Championship and met the second side in a crucial mid-August match. As in the previous season, they won in two days as Worcestershire were dismissed for 94 and 98. Here, D'Oliveira is caught by Richards off the bowling of Jesty. Hampshire took a convincing lead after this match but failed to win any of their final five fixtures, all of which were rain-affected. The final match against Yorkshire at Bournemouth was abandoned without a ball being bowled (the only match to suffer such a fate in the entire country in 1974). Worcestershire took the title by two points.

Trevor Jesty (left) and David Turner (below) made their debuts in successive matches in 1966 and were key members of the successful sides of the 1970s. Both were close to international selection and Jesty was particularly unlucky to make England's one-day side without breaking into Test cricket.

Gordon Greenidge of Hampshire and West Indies. In 1975 he scored 259 against Sussex at Southampton, reaching each fifty and century with a six. The match was vital to Hampshire's chance of winning another Championship, but with Roberts injured they could not dismiss Sussex and finished in third place. They were compensated by winning their first Sunday League title and won another in 1978 when Greenidge scored 637 Sunday League runs at 49 per innings, including a magnificent 122 in the vital victory over Middlesex which brought the title to Hampshire.

England Ladies batting against Hampshire second XI at Southampton in the 1970s. Mike Hill is the wicketkeeper and Australian Peter Ryan is at leg slip.

Desmond Eagar, Hampshire's captain and secretary, was still in office when he died unexpectedly, shortly after the end of the 1977 season. A tireless worker in the Hampshire cause he, as much as any individual, was responsible for the successes of the 1960s and 1970s.

Eight

Cup Winners at Last

Mike Taylor joined Hampshire from Nottinghamshire in time to win a Championship in his first season in 1973. He was also a key member of the Sunday League champions of 1975 and 1978. Having started at the top, he played his last match in 1980 when, curiously, Hampshire were bottom for the first time since 1905. He then became the club's marketing manager, a post he still holds. Here, Mike is presenting a prize in Hampshire's cricket lottery.

Hampshire CCC in 1983. From left to right, back row: Nicholas, C. Smith, Terry, Hussain, Emery, Hardy, Malone, Tremlett, R. Smith, Sainsbury (coach). Front row: Middleton, Goldie, Stevenson, Cowley, Jesty, Pocock, Turner, Southern, Parks, Andrew. Mel Hussain is the elder brother of England captain Nasser Hussain.

Pocock's last side, 1984. He was succeeded by Mark Nicholas which led to the departure of vice-captain Trevor Jesty, who was disappointed at the decision. Greenidge and Marshall were away with the West Indies side and the intriguingly named Elvis Reifer was Hampshire's overseas bowler. From left to right, back row: C. Smith, Maru, Nicholas, Malone, Reifer, Tremlett, Terry. Front row: Cowley, Turner, Pocock, Jesty, Parks.

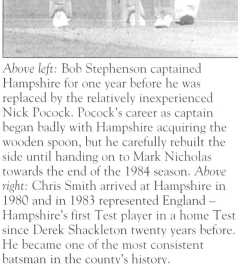

Above left: Bob Stephenson captained Hampshire for one year before he was replaced by the relatively inexperienced Nick Pocock. Pocock's career as captain began badly with Hampshire acquiring the wooden spoon, but he carefully rebuilt the side until handing on to Mark Nicholas towards the end of the 1984 season. *Above right:* Chris Smith arrived at Hampshire in 1980 and in 1983 represented England – Hampshire's first Test player in a home Test since Derek Shackleton twenty years before. He became one of the most consistent batsman in the county's history.

Tim Tremlett is the only major pace bowler produced by Hampshire since Bob Cottam in the early 1960s. Although his career finished somewhat prematurely through injury, he spent the 1990s organising the county's finest youth development programme. Already this has produced promising young cricketers, such as Jason Laney, Derek Kenway, Simon Francis and Lawrence Prittipaul.

One-handed heroes: Lord Tennyson had established a tradition of batting one-handed in Test matches in 1921. In the 1984 series, two Hampshire cricketers, Paul Terry and Malcolm Marshall, were both forced to bat one-handed in successive Tests. Sadly, Terry's innings was the last of a brief international career, although Marshall became one of the great Test players of all time. Both were key members of Mark Nicholas' side which enjoyed so much one-day success.

Mark Nicholas was a charismatic captain and a frequently flamboyant batsman. Here he is at the crease against Sussex in a Benson & Hedges match at Hove.

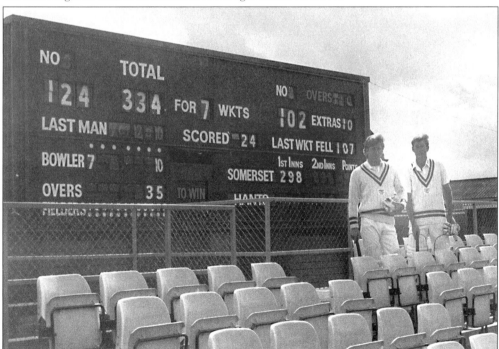

All-rounder Kevan James joined Hampshire from Middlesex in 1985. At Taunton that year he and Tim Tremlett set an eighth-wicket record for the county of 227. This was Tremlett's only first-class century against his father's former county.

Nicholas led Hampshire to second place in the Championship in his first season as captain and in the following year, 1986, they won the Sunday League for the third time. Here, Nicholas holds the John Player Trophy as he receives a cheque from the club's sponsors. The players are, from left to right, back row: Tremlett, James, R. Smith, C. Smith, Turner, Connor. Front row: Greenidge, Cowley, Nicholas, Terry, Parks, Marshall, Bakker.

Hampshire were the last county side to reach a one-day final and when they finally got there the supporters made up for lost time as Hampshire hammered Derbyshire by seven wickets. The success meant that Hampshire's first Championship, first Sunday League and first cup final success were all against Derbyshire. In these pictures the supporters applaud the winning run while the players celebrate on the balcony.

The 1988 Benson & Hedges Cup winners. Left to right, back row: Cowley, C. Smith, Andrew, Ayling, Jefferies, R. Smith, Parks. Front row: Connor, Terry, Nicholas, Turner, James. Kevan James was twelfth man after Portsmouth-born Jon Ayling established himself in his first season. Ayling, Connor, Robin Smith and Terry played in all three of Hampshire's cup finals. Jefferies was Man of the Match in 1988 after he took 5-13 in his 10 overs.

Stephen Jefferies replaced Marshall, who was touring England in 1988. Although he enjoyed relatively little success throughout the season, his match-winning performance at Lord's will never be forgotten; it was, at the time, the best performance in a final at the ground.

The spin twins: Raj Maru arrived from Middlesex in 1984 and is now on the coaching staff, whilst Hampshire-born Shaun Udal represented England in 10 one-day internationals in 1994/95 and is currently vice-captain.

Tony Middleton waited patiently for his chance in the Hampshire side and when it arrived he took it splendidly, winning two cup-winners' medals and an England 'A' tour to Australia. His career batting average places him in the top ten Hampshire batsmen of all-time. He is currently a member of Hampshire's coaching staff.

David Gower joined Hampshire from Leicestershire in 1990 and scored 145 on his Championship debut versus Sussex. He captained Hampshire in the 1991 NatWest final and left at the end of 1994, telling his captain and friend Mark Nicholas: 'To be honest, I've had enough.' He has swapped positions since this photograph was taken and is now a leading media figure in the world of cricket.

Hampshire reached their first 60-over final in 1991 and won a thrilling victory against Surrey. The Hampshire squad for that year was, from left to right, back row: Taylor, Morris, Udal, Turner, Shine, Thursfield, Flint, Cox. Middle row: Tremlett (coach), Aymes, Aqib Javed, James, Bakker, Ayling, Middleton, Connor, Sainsbury (coach). Front row: Maru, Gower, Terry, Nicholas, C. Smith, Parks, R. Smith, Wood.

The winning balcony in 1991. David Gower captained Hampshire after Mark Nicholas suffered a broken finger from a ball from Waqar Younis in the previous county match. Tony Middleton made his debut in the competition after Chris Smith's premature retirement just weeks earlier and made a fine half-century.

Hampshire made a swift return to Lord's ten months later for their second successful Benson & Hedges Cup final. Kevan James and coach Tim Tremlett are pictured arriving at the ground on the first morning.

The excitement of this third final was somewhat reduced when rain on the Saturday forced the game into a second day. With Kent struggling on 114-4, Udal is shown bowling from the pavilion end in front of a somewhat sparse crowd.

Despite loyal service since 1979, Malcolm Marshall had only won a solitary Sunday League medal before his appearance in the 1992 final. He made a vital early breakthrough when Trevor Ward was caught by Bob Parks for 5 and finished with 3-33. In this photograph, Marshall and Parks are being congratulated by Nicholas, Middleton, Terry, Smith and Udal.

More balcony celebrations as Marshall waves to the crowd, toasted by Connor, Nicholas, Maru and Udal, while below Nicholas appears overwhelmed as Raj makes proper use of the bubbly.

Mark Nicholas' sides won four one-day competitions in seven seasons, but in the Championship never bettered the second place of his first season in charge. Through the 1990s major players like Marshall, Gower, Chris Smith, Terry, Parks and Nicholas himself departed. Too few young players came through to replace them, signings from other counties generally disappointed and a number of overseas signings failed to fill Marshall's boots as Hampshire struggled. Of this 1993 side, Gower, Marshall, Ayling, Shine, Turner, Wood and Byrne departed before the following season. By the year 2000 only four players – Laney, Aymes, Udal and Robin Smith – remained.

Nine

Movements and Departures

Mark Nicholas leads his Hampshire side out after tea for their last ever home match at Dean Park on 20 August 1992. The game against Middlesex ended in a draw despite a fine all-round performance by Jon Ayling (57 and match figures of 7-49). Hampshire did return to the ground in 1998 when they were drawn away against Dorset in the NatWest Trophy.

Malcolm Marshall returned as coach and John Stephenson arrived from Essex and was appointed captain in 1996, a reign that was to last just two years. His first squad, from left to right, back row: Kendall, Bovill, White, Francis, Botham, Dibden, Milburn. Middle row: Marshall, Treagus, Whitaker, Morris, Benjamin, Thursfield, James, Renshaw, Keech, Laney, Tremlett (coach). Front row: Thomas, Aymes, Maru, Smith, Stephenson, Terry, Connor, Udal, Garaway.

On the field, the mid-1990s were an unhappy time for Hampshire but behind the scenes important developments were under way. The county were awarded a National Lottery grant in excess of £7 million towards the development of a new ground and sporting village at West End in the borough of Eastleigh. Holding the cheque are the principal people involved in this development: Mike Taylor (marketing manager), Bill Hughes (vice-chairman), Tony Baker (chief executive), Brian Ford (chairman) and Wilfrid Weld (president). Below, Mark Nicholas, Robin Smith and Shaun Udal join a local resident in a toast on the site of the new ground.

Many counties concentrated their cricket on fewer grounds as festival weeks decreased through the 1990s. Hampshire announced that they would play no more cricket on the Portsmouth (above) and Basingstoke (below) grounds after the 2000 season.

Matthew Hayden joined Hampshire for just one year, 1997, but he was a popular and successful player. Here, he receives a cheque from Mike Taylor to mark his achievement in outscoring all other county batsmen in the Sunday League during that season.

Robin Smith won 62 Test caps between 1988 and 1996 and when he was omitted still had the best Test batting average of any current England batsman. His total of England Test caps far exceeds that of any other Hampshire player and he also appeared in 71 limited-overs internationals. Here he joins Graeame Hick in celebrating a rare England victory abroad – at Barbados in 1994.

Robin Smith succeeded John Stephenson as captain of Hampshire in 1998 and they enjoyed one of their better seasons of recent years, finishing in the top half of both leagues and reaching a NatWest semi-final. Here, Smith holds the bat used by E.G. Wynyard as Hampshire's captain 100 years before.

Smith's first squad, 1998. From left to right, back row: Laney, White, Makin, Francis, Dibden, Loudon, Kendall, Kenway. Middle row: Marshall (coach), Haynes (coach), Keech, Hartley, Hansen, Renshaw, Savident, A. Morris, Mascarenhas, Z. Morris, Tremlett (coach). Front row: Whitaker, Aymes, James, Udal, Smith, Maru, Connor, Stephenson, Garaway.

Dimitri Mascarenhas enjoyed a marvellous season in 1998. He was awarded his county cap and was voted Young Cricketer of the Year by Hampshire Exiles. He was unlucky not to win a place in the England 'A' side.

Floodlit competitive cricket arrived in England and Hampshire's first appearance under floodlights was at Edgbaston where they won a thrilling victory, which helped to secure them a place in the new first division.

With the introduction of the new National League in 1999, counties adopted nicknames and mascots. Hampshire were known as the Hawks and were accompanied by a mascot named 'Harry the Hawk' who amused the children but brought little luck as Hampshire were relegated. The playing squad with Harry is, from left to right, back row: Keech, Hamblin, Francis, Loudon, Kendall, White, Kenway. Middle row: Z. Morris, Lugsden, Hansen, Savident, Renshaw, A. Morris, Mascarenhas, Garaway. Front row: Laney, Aymes, Udal, Smith, James, Stephenson, Hartley. James retired at the end of his fifteenth season with Hampshire.

Hampshire take the field for their first home match in the 45-over National League against Kent. The players' pavilion is the oldest building on the ground at Northlands Road.

Cardigan Connor also announced his retirement early in the 1999 season and returned to his native Anguila. With the retirement of Malcolm Marshall as coach and the decision to replace Nixon McLean with Shane Warne, 2000 was likely to be the first season since Roy Marshall arrived in 1953 that there would be no Caribbean connection with Hampshire.

James Adams, an outstanding young batsman, receives his award as the under-19 Player of the Season in the 1998 side. He joined Hampshire on a summer contract in 2000.

In 1998, Hampshire's under-19 side, managed by former batsman Barry Reed, won their national competition. A number of their young players then featured in a successful Hampshire Board XI in 1999 and by the end of that year one member of the side, Lawrence Prittipaul, had made his first team debut. Here, Jon Ayling and Prittipaul listen to a point made by Barry Reed. All three Hampshire cricketers were born in Portsmouth. Following his premature retirement, Ayling has become a successful coach.

Will Kendall and Derek Kenway leave the field at Lord's with the award-winning media centre in the background. Both players enjoyed their best season in 1999 and Kendall was rewarded with his county cap.

The World Cup came to England in 1999. Southampton was selected as a host venue and Hampshire also entertained England in a warm-up game. In a photocall before the match, two 'Anglo-Aussies', Dimitri Mascarenhas and Alan Mullally, greet each other. At the end of that season Mullally left Leicestershire to rejoin Hampshire, his first county.

At the end of the 1999 season the County Championship was divided into two divisions for the first time in its history. Hampshire went into the final day of their season at Derby knowing that only a victory would guarantee them a place in the first division. After a day of fluctuating fortunes they won an enthralling contest by just 2 runs when Peter Hartley caught and bowled the last man. Here, Hartley and his captain Robin Smith leave the field at the close of the game. Smith had enjoyed better fortune than A.H. Wood (below), who was Hampshire's captain when they were 'relegated' to second-class status in the previous century.

Southampton-born Adie Aymes was Hampshire's beneficiary in 2000 and one of their finest ever wicketkeepers. He is the 'keeper with the highest career batting average. He is seen here in action against Australia in 1997, keeping wicket as Mark Waugh moves towards a century (right) and making top score in Hampshire's first innings (below).

Old and new: the pavilions at Northlands Road (above) which will be demolished at the end of the 2000 season and Hampshire's new West End ground taking shape during 1999 (below).

Ten
Malcolm Marshall
1958-1999

Malcolm Marshall returned to Hampshire as coach but in the early part of 1999 he was diagnosed with cancer and died in November of that year. He was one of the greatest cricketers ever to play for the county and one of the most good-natured men. He is pictured above leaving the field on his last appearance at Northlands Road in 1994 when he led his own West Indies XI against Hampshire. In the bottom photograph he is bowling to his son Mali during the tea interval of his last visit to Northlands Road on 10 September 1999.